I0877755

The Study Guide to the Encyclical Letter of Pope Francis

THE STUDY GUIDE TO THE Encyclical Letter OF Pope Francis

Fratelli Tutti, On Fraternity and Social Friendship

BY MARCUS MESCHER

Paulist Press
New York / Mahwah, NJ

The Scripture quotations contained herein are from the New Revised Standard Version: Catholic Edition, Copyright © 1989 and 1993, by the Division of Christian Education of the National Council of the Churches of Christ in the United States of America. Used by permission. All rights reserved.

Cover image by Jozef Sedmak / Dreamstime.com
Cover and book design by Lynn Else

Fratelli tutti, copyright © 2020 by Libreria Editrice Vaticana
00120 Città del Vaticano
www.libreriaeditricevaticana.va
All rights reserved.
Reprinted by arrangement with Libreria Editrice Vaticana

Study material copyright © 2021 by Marcus Mescher

All rights reserved. No part of this publication may be reproduced, stored in a retrieval system, or transmitted in any form or by any means, electronic, mechanical, photocopying, recording, scanning, or otherwise, without either the prior written permission of the Publisher, or authorization through payment of the appropriate per-copy fee to the Copyright Clearance Center, Inc., www.copyright.com. Requests to the Publisher for permission should be addressed to the Permissions Department, Paulist Press, permissions@paulistpress.com.

Library of Congress Control Number: 2021937905

ISBN 978-0-8091-5565-1 (paperback)
ISBN 978-1-58768-964-2 (e-book)

Published by Paulist Press
997 Macarthur Boulevard
Mahwah, New Jersey 07430
www.paulistpress.com

Printed and bound in the
United States of America

CONTENTS

PREFACE

A Spirituality for Solidarity

Solidarity is the focal theme of Pope Francis's 2020 encyclical, *Fratelli Tutti* ("On Fraternity and Social Friendship"). Solidarity is more than an exhortation to inclusion or an appeal to unity; it is the fruit of faith in God-who-is-mercy (Exod 34:6–7). Throughout his pontificate, Francis has emphasized that God is revealed through the experience of mercy, and that "mercy is God's identity card."[1] Mercy represents the summation of what God wants for and from us, the defining characteristic for Christian discipleship (Matt 9:13). Mercy means more than loving kindness; it also implies tenderness, fidelity, forgiveness, fortitude.[2] It inspires personal virtues like humility, patience, and generosity and also a shared commitment to practice solidarity as a church called to be both a "house of communion" and a "house that welcomes all."[3] Just as the etymology of the word *catholic* connotes universality, the church serves as a sacrament of God's mercy and solidarity with us.[4] This relationship between mercy and solidarity is also a reason for hope, stretching our imagination to prayerfully consider what *more* God can make possible for us and through us.

In this spirit, *Fratelli Tutti* addresses a world marred by countless examples of social distrust and division, unjust inequalities, and temptations to despair. It reads like a love letter from a shepherd to his flock, revealing both his awareness of the struggles they face as well as his encouragement to be witnesses of faith, hope, and love. This encyclical offers a robust reflection on contemporary challenges and opportunities to live up to the command to "love your neighbor as yourself" (Lev 19:18; Mark 12:31; Matt 22:39; Luke 10:27). In the opening paragraphs of *Fratelli Tutti*, Pope Francis explains his intention in writing this document:

> I offer this social Encyclical as a modest contribution to continued reflection, in the hope that in the face of present-day attempts to eliminate or ignore others, we may prove capable of responding with a new vision of fraternity and social friendship that will not remain at the level of words. Although I have written it from the Christian convictions that inspire and sustain me, I have sought to make this reflection an invitation to dialogue among all people of good will. (no. 6)

Francis notes that the global spread of the coronavirus helped shape his focus on solidarity and spurred his sense of urgency to address the problems both caused and exposed by this pandemic. COVID-19 is a sobering reminder that we are impacted by the decisions others make just as others are affected by the decisions we make. Global problems cannot be solved by random acts of kindness; we need to harness our moral imagination and moral will to collectively reflect and pray, discuss and discern, strategize and mobilize as partners who share in a ministry of love that does justice for all. Pope Francis presents *Fratelli Tutti* as a resource for personal and social transformation, aiming to inspire the significant changes we need to resist the "functionalistic and privatized mindset that inexorably leads to a 'throwaway culture'" (no. 188) impeding our ability to see ourselves as equal members belonging to a "single family dwelling in a common home" (no. 17). His stress on solidarity is a response to the social fragility and fragmentation that makes it "more difficult to resolve problems that affect us all," adding that "anyone who thinks that the only lesson to be learned was the need to improve what we were already doing, or to refine existing systems and regulations, is denying reality" (no. 7). *Fratelli Tutti* provides us an important opportunity to become more aware of reality so we can take greater responsibility for restoring it. Pope Francis calls on us to "dream together" about who we want to be on the other side of the COVID-19 pandemic, to discover and become sources of "renewed hope" (nos. 8, 55). Solidarity requires that we defy self-interest and narrow concerns; he insists, "No one is saved alone; we can only be saved together" (nos. 32, 54, 137). As bishop of Rome, he calls on the church—simultaneously a local and global reality—to witness mercy, solidarity, and hope by cultivating "artisans of peace" among its members (no. 284). He proposes that our communities in crisis can be healed by practicing inclusive concern, mutual respect, and a shared commitment to the common good.

WHAT IS SOLIDARITY?

The title of *Fratelli Tutti* comes from the "Admonitions" of St. Francis of Assisi (whom the pope aims to emulate by taking the name Francis), as he addressed his fellow Christians: "brothers and sisters all." In this encyclical, the pope depicts solidarity as an expression of the bonds of filiation from "sharing the same flesh, as children of the same earth which is our common home" (no. 8). However, *Fratelli Tutti* employs the gendered term *fraternity* and fails to include any women among its 288 citations.[5] Language matters because it expresses and also creates meaning; because *fraternity* does not recognize the presence and participation of women, this study guide intentionally uses the word *solidarity* as a more inclusive term for conveying the bonds of "fraternity" or expressions of "fraternal love."

The word *solidarity* might give some people the impression of being ideologically inspired (as a leftist political agenda, for example), but it is rooted in the biblical vision of being faithful to the demands of God's covenant with Israel (Gen 15:18). Fidelity to God is expressed through caring for all members of the community, pursuing right-relationships that reflect justice (*tsedaqah*) and peace (*shalom*). Justice and peace result from social solidarity and environmental sustainability in promoting the fullness of life for all, the flourishing of every member of God's creation.[6] This includes a special preference and priority for the marginalized and vulnerable.[7] Pope John Paul II calls solidarity an "undoubtedly Christian virtue" because it reflects the merciful, inclusive love of Jesus's teaching and healing ministry (*Sollicitudo Rei Socialis* 40). When solidarity is integrated into individual attitudes and actions and characterizes communities, we live up to our vocation in belonging to "one body" (1 Cor 12:1–31) as God's ambassadors of reconciliation in the world (2 Cor 5:18–21).[8] Insofar as "Christ is all and in all" (Col 3:11), we have a duty to see Christ in the other, be Christ for and with the other, and moreover, to recognize and affirm each other as "God's co-workers" (1 Cor 3:9 NABRE). Solidarity affirms that we are equal in dignity and responsibility; it results from loving our neighbors. As Pope Francis has asserted, "love has no alibi," meaning that no one is excused from these repeated commands to care for others and work to restore bonds broken by personal and social sin.[9]

Although solidarity is a key principle of Catholic social teaching, it often gets reduced to a benign platitude like unity or togetherness. As a moral virtue and moral principle, solidarity carries a greater costliness than we might like to acknowledge. Solidarity goes unmentioned in Pope Francis's first encyclical, *Lumen Fidei* ("The Light of Faith"), published in 2013 in collaboration with his predecessor, Pope Emeritus Benedict XVI. But this document underscores that the "history of faith, from its inception, has been a history of fraternity" (no. 54). Francis explains,

> As the history of salvation proceeds, man discovers that God wants everyone to participate, as brothers, in the one blessing, which finds its fullness in Jesus, so that all may become one. The inexhaustible love of the Father is communicated to us, in Jesus, also through the presence of the brother. Faith teaches us to see that in every man there is a blessing for me, that the light of the face of God illuminates me through the face of the brother. How many benefits has the gaze of the Christian faith brought to the city of men for their common life! (no. 54)

Solidarity witnesses that every human person is made in God's image and likeness, all members of God's single family (Gen 1:26–27). In his 2015 encyclical, *Laudato Si'* ("On Care for Our Common Home"), Francis urged Catholics and all people of good will to undergo an "ecological conversion" in response to the cry of the earth (no. 5). "Everything is connected," Pope Francis insists (91, 117), requiring a "new and universal solidarity" (no. 14).[10] Solidarity is also to be considered longitudinally, given the implications for our duties to future generations (nos. 95, 109, 159–62). *Fratelli Tutti* acknowledges that solidarity "has become a dirty word" in some contexts, especially as a threat to individual freedom or suggesting coercion or conformity in a top-down exercise of power (no. 116). Nevertheless, Pope Francis stresses that solidarity is a moral duty, requiring more than occasional acts of service. Highlighting solidarity as inclusive belonging produced through drawing close to others (no. 30), Pope Francis describes a vision for building a "community of belonging and solidarity" (no. 36) through a "culture of encounter" (no. 216) that not only brings people together across differences, but works to dismantle unjust inequalities in social, economic, political, and ecological arenas.

This is important because Pope Francis presents solidarity as a corrective against unilateral charity that can reinforce self-righteousness or condescending pity. Charity is asymmetrical; it casts some people as donors and others as recipients. Such a framework renders some individuals as passively waiting on the goodwill of others, fostering a dependence that strips them of their desires and agency. Moreover, it risks sending the message that social problems can be solved by individual generosity. Giving a few dollars to someone experiencing homelessness is a kind gesture, but it does nothing to help the root causes of homelessness, including but not limited to a lack of access to affordable housing, quality education, job placement services, nutrition, healthcare, counseling, or substance abuse treatment. Similarly, charity cannot accomplish what justice requires. Justice involves action and advocacy for equity between persons as well as equitable access to resources and full participation in social, economic, and political arenas. Justice demands humane exercises of power across individuals and institutions. To be just persons and build just communities, we have to analyze how power is exercised and confront forces that dehumanize, divide, and deprive. Justice requires that we speak and act, vote and organize in a way that defends human dignity and rights, and advances freedom and responsibility for integral development, sustainability, solidarity, and peace. It also obliges us to undo the beliefs and practices, systems and structures that foment degradation, fear, prejudice, selfishness, and greed, exacerbate inequality, undermine peace in our communities, and desensitize us to violence. Moreover, restorative justice is owed to those who have been denied their dignity and rights. In the face of an unjust status quo, our silence, ambiguity, and neutrality become obstacles to justice.

To be clear, it is a false choice to favor either charity or justice. The church has long taught that charity and justice are complementary duties.[11] Solidarity holds charity and justice together, combining generosity in order to meet immediate needs with advocating for the establishment of more inclusive, equitable, and empowering systems and structures. Equality and mutuality distinguish solidarity from charity; solidarity is the practice of universal love striving for the reciprocal support and accountability of genuine communion. Solidarity is the habit of loving God by loving our neighbors both near and far; it is an expression of social holiness.

Another reason why solidarity is not reducible to unity or togetherness is because it resists any in-group or out-group distinction as expressed by categories of "us" and "them." In the canon of Catholic social teaching, the popular definition of *solidarity* comes from Pope John Paul II's 1987 encyclical, *Sollicitudo Rei Socialis* ("On Social Concerns"): "A firm and persevering determination to commit oneself to the common good; that is to say to the good of all and of each individual, because we are all really responsible for all" (no. 38). On the one hand, this is helpful because it reminds us that our duties to others are not contingent on shared beliefs or values. On the other hand, defining solidarity as an orientation to the common good can make it difficult to know what distinguishes these two tenets of Catholic social teaching. Pope John Paul II traces solidarity back to the discussion of the "bonds of friendship" and "brotherly love" in Pope Leo XIII's 1891 encyclical, *Rerum Novarum* ("On the Condition of Labor"), typically listed as the first encyclical in the body of Catholic social teaching.[12] Pope John Paul II invoked solidarity in seeking harmony between the internal order of each nation and international order, envisioning interdependence on "the moral plane" as an essential condition for integral human development and peace (*Sollicitudo Rei Socialis* 26, 39). Solidarity therefore serves as a moral principle for social, systemic, and structural application; for example, it demands that we establish policies and practices to ensure the just distribution of goods and services in addition to sacrificing self-interest to deliver on the rights of the most vulnerable.

Solidarity is also a moral virtue: an attitude that shapes our habits and thus forms our moral character. Solidarity represents a mean between extremes of collectivism and individualism; it is oriented toward inclusion and an interdependence honoring human dignity, advancing human freedom and rights by exercising duties to the well-being of others, especially those in greatest need. *Sollicitudo Rei Socialis* defines *solidarity* as the personal disposition that inspires the social expression of loving one's neighbor with "total gratuity, forgiveness and reconciliation" (no. 40). The *Catechism of the Catholic Church* teaches that solidarity is a practice of "social charity" and "friendship," expanding love from the interpersonal level to the social and structural levels, going as far as claiming that "international solidarity is a requirement of the moral order; world peace depends in part upon this" (nos. 1939, 1941). Whereas friendship might inspire an image of two friends who delight in each other, support each other, and hold each other accountable, solidarity is the social expression of friendship marked by mutual respect and tender care, honesty and generosity, reciprocal loyalty and trust in the spirit of equality and coresponsibility on the individual, interpersonal, and institutional levels.

FRATELLI TUTTI AND CONSCIENCE FORMATION

Fratelli Tutti is the latest addition to the body of Catholic social teaching. Catholic social teaching draws from Scripture, Tradition, natural law, and human experience in order to issue normative statements on fulfilling the social mission of the church. It comprises a collection of papal and episcopal writing, typically beginning with Pope Leo XIII's 1891 encyclical, *Rerum Novarum* ("On the Condition of Labor"). Over the last 130 years, successive popes and bishops' conferences have added to this library of social doctrine, attesting to the "permanent value of the Church's teaching" as "always living and active."[13] The church prides itself as an "expert in humanity," offering insight into the conditions necessary for defending human dignity and rights (*Sollicitudo Rei Socialis* 7). As authoritative doctrine, Catholic social teaching should be given a presumption of truth; as a moral guide, these normative claims should be integrated into the daily life of Christian individuals and communities.

Popes write encyclicals to teach the lay faithful about the demands of Christian discipleship. Catholic social teaching draws on encyclicals and other pastoral letters to inform our conscience as part of the formation of each individual's moral identity and perception, agency and relationships. The *Catechism of the Catholic Church* states that by virtue of our conscience, every individual can hear the voice of God calling us to "love and to do what is good and to avoid evil" (no. 1776). The conscience is our "most secret core" and "sanctuary," serving as the "Vicar of Christ" (nos. 1776, 1778). Conscience is not the same as "going with your gut"; it is an innate capacity and never-ending activity. Conscience formation is a life-long process to help us grow in love for what is right, true, good, and just so that it becomes like second nature to us. Our conscience does not prevent us from making mistakes, but it does task us with learning from the times when we misuse our free will. Pope Francis reminds us, "Christian morality is not a never falling down, but an always getting up."[14] Catholic social teaching is designed to give us access to moral wisdom to keep developing our capacity to know and do what love and justice require of us.

The word *conscience* means "to know together," pointing to the dialogical (i.e., shared) work to consult Scripture, Tradition, natural law, and human experience thanks to the virtue of prudence and "the help of the Holy Spirit" (no. 1788). Since no single individual can fully grasp the truth alone, we are morally responsible to pursue moral growth by seeking counsel from others. Conscience formation is a personal and communal discipline, which means that as we deepen what we "know together," we equip and empower our conscience to order and interpret truth claims, exercise the virtue of prudence, and make moral judgments so we can speak and act accordingly.[15] Just as we are called to honor our conscience, so too, we must respect the consciences of our neighbors.

The process of moral discernment has sometimes been labeled as See-Judge-Act, often associated with Belgian priest Joseph Cardijn. *Fratelli Tutti* both reflects and informs the See-Judge-Act method of social analysis, ethical reflection, and just action. This is an important process of bringing faith to life and life to faith. The structure of *Fratelli Tutti*—

with its opening chapter studying the "dark clouds over a closed world," the second chapter focusing on the story of the Samaritan in Luke 10:25–37, and subsequent chapters dedicated to inspire a response in universal love—follows this pattern of social analysis, theological reflection, and pastoral planning. Each reader is called and empowered to read "the signs of the times" (Matt 16:3), reflect on and pray about what God requires from and for us, and then think, feel, speak, and act as agents of love and justice.

The See-Judge-Act approach has been further developed into a "pastoral spiral," as proposed by Joe Holland and Peter Henriot.[16] As the name implies, the process of social analysis, moral formation, and exercising social responsibility is an unending cycle guided by these five steps:

1. Insertion: become aware of the lived experience of individuals and communities from a particular social location.
2. Social analysis: examine root causes and consequences of pressing social problems, find connections, identify those who are responsible for making decisions, and assess who benefits and suffers as a result.
3. Theological reflection: reflect on, pray with, and discuss how Scripture and church teaching address how to love God, self, and others in light of these circumstances.
4. Pastoral response: collaborate in determining short- and long-term goals and strategies—bridging together the micro and macro levels—to meet the needs of the people involved.
5. Evaluation: gauge the effectiveness of the response and imagine new possibilities for the future.

In light of this process of moral discernment and conscience formation, *Fratelli Tutti* should not only be read and studied; it should be the subject of prayer and conversation. Moving beyond a discussion of its credibility and meaning, we should become more attentive and responsive to the condition of human dignity, the status of human rights, the qualities of our relationships, and the health of our communities. Social problems are spiritual problems because they point to our failures to use our free will, personally and collectively. Pope Francis presents this encyclical to, as the *Catechism* describes, assist in the "education of conscience [which] is indispensable for human beings who are subjected to negative influences and tempted by sin to prefer their own judgment and to reject authoritative teachings" (no. 1783). *Fratelli Tutti* challenges us to confront the causes of personal and social sin by detecting ignorance and indifference, insufficient action or harmful systems. Pope Francis invites us to a courageous and compassionate examination of conscience to be on guard against deception and fear, selfishness and complacency, suspicion and scorn, exclusion and judgment, shame and guilt. He adds to the canon of Catholic social teaching to encourage us to respond with mercy, solidarity, and hope on the individual, interpersonal, and institutional levels.

HOW TO USE THIS STUDY GUIDE

This study guide is designed to help readers navigate Pope Francis's insightful and inspiring encyclical on solidarity. Following this preface, the encyclical largely speaks for itself, so you can freely and fully immerse yourself in it. Each chapter of the encyclical is introduced with a brief synopsis to frame Pope Francis's overall message, noting key themes to help orient your approach. Some passages are highlighted for your special attention. At the conclusion of each chapter, you will find questions intended to spark your reflection, analysis, and possibilities for application. At the end of this volume, you can also find recommendations for further reading as well as resources for advocacy and action. This study guide aims to steer you through the pastoral spiral so you can feel more equipped to respond to our call to be "God's co-workers" (1 Cor 3:9 NABRE) in healing a wounded world.

Notes

1. Pope Francis, *The Name of God Is Mercy*, trans. Oonagh Stransky (New York: Random House, 2016), 9.

2. The biblical words for mercy (*hesed* and *eleos*) appear over two hundred times, illustrating many dimensions to the experience—and demands—of mercy. See, e.g., Exod 34:6–7; Lev 19:2; Deut 15:4–7; Josh 2:12; 1 Sam 20:14–17; 2 Sam 7:11–16; Ps 72:1–4; Isa 54:8–10; Hos 2:16–21; Mic 7:19; Matt 9:13; Mark 5:19; Luke 6:36; Jas 3:17.

3. Pope Francis, *The Church of Mercy: A Vision for the Church* (Chicago: Loyola Press, 2014), 26–32.

4. In his 2015 apostolic letter *Misericordiae Vultus* (to announce the Extraordinary Jubilee of Mercy), Pope Francis offers an extended reflection on mercy as the "wellspring of joy, serenity, and peace," the basis for our salvation, the "ultimate and supreme act by which God comes to meet us," and "the bridge that connects God and man, opening our hearts to the hope of being loved forever despite our sinfulness" (no. 2).

5. The lone woman cited in the document is Jesus's mother, Mary (nos. 276 and 278).

6. See, e.g., Exod 19:3–6; 22:21–23; Lev 19:18; 25:23–43; Deut 10:17–19; 24:17–22; Tob 4:6–11; Isa 1:16–17; 58:6–7; Jer 7:5–7; 22:13–16; 29:4–7; Mic 6:8; Zech 7:9–10; 8:16.

7. See, e.g., Exod 23:11; Lev 19:9–10; Deut 15:4–11; Job 34:20–28; Prov 31:8–9; Sir 4:8–10; Isa 58:6–7; Matt 25:31–46; Luke 4:16–21; 6:20–23; Acts 4:32–35; 20:32–35; Jas 2:1–6, 14–17; 5:1–6; 1 John 3:17–18.

8. See also Rom 12:3–21; Gal 3:28; Eph 2:11–22; Heb 13:1–2.

9. Pope Francis, "First World Day of the Poor Message," November 19, 2017, http://www.vatican.va/content/francesco/en/messages/poveri/documents/papa-francesco_20170613_messaggio-i-giornatamondiale-poveri-2017.html.

10. Even before God's covenant with Abraham, God's covenant with Noah and his descendants also makes all living creatures of the earth our covenant partners (Gen 9:9–17), explicitly conferring an ecological dimension to solidarity.

11. See, e.g., *Catechism of the Catholic Church* 1889, 2437–49; *Quadragesimo Anno* 218; *Gaudium et Spes* 69; *Populorum Progressio* 44; *Familiaris Consortio* 43; *Sollicitudo Rei Socialis* 42; *Deus Caritas Est* 26–29; *Caritas in Veritate* 6–7.

12. See Pope John Paul II, *Centesimus Annus* 10; Pope Leo XIII, *Rerum Novarum* 25.

13. *Catechism of the Catholic Church* 2421.

14. Pope Francis, "Address to the Communion and Liberation Movement," March 7, 2015, http://www.vatican.va/content/francesco/en/speeches/2015/march/documents/papa-francesco_20150307_comunione-liberazione.html.

15. For an accessible discussion of this process, see the chapter on conscience by Bernard V. Brady in *Be Good & Do Good: Thinking Through Moral Theology* (Maryknoll, NY: Orbis Books, 2014), 141–68.

16. Joe Holland and Peter Henriot, *Social Analysis: Linking Faith and Justice* (Maryknoll, NY: Orbis Books, 1983), 8–9.

INTRODUCTION

SYNOPSIS

In eight brief paragraphs, Pope Francis outlines his objective for *Fratelli Tutti*. The opening lines are inspired by his namesake, St. Francis of Assisi, in whose "Admonitions" he calls on his "brothers and sisters" to live "marked by the flavour of the Gospel" (no. 1). Building on St. Francis's vision of kinship with all creation, Pope Francis references his 2015 encyclical, *Laudato Si'*, as a prologue for this extended reflection on the obstacles and opportunities for solidarity with all, and especially the poor, vulnerable, and excluded. Pope Francis also highlights the interfaith commitments that St. Francis modeled in his visit to Egypt to dialogue with the Sultan Malik-el-Kamil during the Crusades. The pope recounts his own efforts in ecumenism with Orthodox Patriarch Bartholomew and interreligious collaboration with the Grand Imam Ahmad Al-Tayyeb as concrete examples of the kind of "culture of encounter" necessary for mutual respect, greater understanding, co-responsibility, reconciliation, and peace. In his 2013 apostolic exhortation, *Evangellii Gaudium* ("The Joy of the Gospel"), Pope Francis described this commitment as a response to

> the Gospel [that] tells us constantly to run the risk of a face-to-face encounter with others, with their physical presence which challenges us, with their pain and their pleas, with their joy which infects us in our close and continuous interaction. True faith in the incarnate Son of God is inseparable from self-giving, from membership in the community, from service, from reconciliation with others. The Son of God, by becoming flesh, summoned us to the revolution of tenderness. (no. 88)

In concluding the introduction to *Fratelli Tutti*, Pope Francis reminds us that dreams are "built together" and urges us to embrace this moment in history—as we navigate life in and after a global pandemic—to "dream together," to imagine and give voice to who we hope to become and how we can build a world where we recognize one another as equals in dignity and belonging to one another as "brothers and sisters all" (no. 8).

---

1. "Fratelli tutti."[1] With these words, Saint Francis of Assisi addressed his brothers and sisters and proposed to them a way of life marked by the flavour of the Gospel. Of the counsels Francis offered, I would like to select the one in which he calls for a love that transcends the barriers of geography and distance, and declares blessed all those who love their brother "as much when he is far away from him as when he is with him."[2] In his simple and direct way, Saint Francis expressed the essence of a fraternal openness that allows us to acknowledge, appreciate and love each person, regardless of physical proximity, regardless of where he or she was born or lives.

1. *Admonitions*, 6, 1. English translation in *Francis of Assisi: Early Documents*, vol 1., New York, London, Manila (1999), 131.
2. Ibid., 25: op. cit., 136.

2. This saint of fraternal love, simplicity and joy, who inspired me to write the Encyclical *Laudato Si'*, prompts me once more to devote this new Encyclical to fraternity and social friendship. Francis felt himself a brother to the sun, the sea and the wind, yet he knew that he was even closer to those of his own flesh. Wherever he went, he sowed seeds of peace and walked alongside the poor, the abandoned, the infirm and the outcast, the least of his brothers and sisters.

WITHOUT BORDERS

3. There is an episode in the life of Saint Francis that shows his openness of heart, which knew no bounds and transcended differences of origin, nationality, colour or religion. It was his visit to Sultan Malik-el-Kamil, in Egypt, which entailed considerable hardship, given Francis' poverty, his scarce resources, the great distances to be traveled and their differences of language, culture and religion. That journey, undertaken at the time of the Crusades, further demonstrated the breadth and grandeur of his love, which sought to embrace everyone. Francis' fidelity to his Lord was commensurate with his love for his brothers and sisters. Unconcerned for the hardships and dangers involved, Francis went to meet the Sultan with the same attitude that he instilled in his disciples: if they found themselves "among the Saracens and other nonbelievers," without renouncing their own identity they were not to "engage in arguments or disputes, but to be subject to every human creature for God's sake."[3] In the context of the times, this was an extraordinary recommendation. We are impressed that some eight hundred years ago Saint Francis urged that all forms of hostility or conflict be avoided and that a humble and fraternal "subjection" be shown to those who did not share his faith.

4. Francis did not wage a war of words aimed at imposing doctrines; he simply spread the love of God. He understood that

---

3. Saint Francis of Assisi, *Earlier Rule of the Friars Minor* (*Regula non bullata*), 16: 3.6: op. cit. 74.

"God is love and those who abide in love abide in God" (1 *Jn* 4:16). In this way, he became a father to all and inspired the vision of a fraternal society. Indeed, "only the man who approaches others, not to draw them into his own life, but to help them become ever more fully themselves, can truly be called a father."[4] In the world of that time, bristling with watchtowers and defensive walls, cities were a theatre of brutal wars between powerful families, even as poverty was spreading through the countryside. Yet there Francis was able to welcome true peace into his heart and free himself of the desire to wield power over others. He became one of the poor and sought to live in harmony with all. Francis has inspired these pages.

5. Issues of human fraternity and social friendship have always been a concern of mine. In recent years, I have spoken of them repeatedly and in different settings. In this Encyclical, I have sought to bring together many of those statements and to situate them in a broader context of reflection. In the preparation of *Laudato Si'*, I had a source of inspiration in my brother Bartholomew, the Orthodox Patriarch, who has spoken forcefully of our need to care for creation. In this case, I have felt particularly encouraged by the Grand Imam Ahmad Al-Tayyeb, with whom I met in Abu Dhabi, where we declared that "God has created all human beings equal in rights, duties and dignity, and has called them to live together as brothers and sisters."[5] This was no mere diplomatic gesture, but a reflection born of dialogue and common commitment. The present Encyclical takes up and develops some of the great themes raised in the Document that we both signed. I have also incorporated, along with my own thoughts, a number of letters, documents and considerations that I have received from many individuals and groups throughout the world.

6. The following pages do not claim to offer a complete teaching on fraternal love, but rather to consider its universal scope, its openness to every man and woman. I offer this social

---

4. Eloi Leclerc, O.F.M., *Exil et tendresse*, Éd. Franciscaines, Paris, 1962, 205.

5. *Document on Human Fraternity for World Peace and Living Together*, Abu Dhabi (4 February 2019): *L'Osservatore Romano*, 4–5 February 2019, p. 6.

Encyclical as a modest contribution to continued reflection, in the hope that in the face of present-day attempts to eliminate or ignore others, we may prove capable of responding with a new vision of fraternity and social friendship that will not remain at the level of words. Although I have written it from the Christian convictions that inspire and sustain me, I have sought to make this reflection an invitation to dialogue among all people of good will.

7. As I was writing this letter, the Covid-19 pandemic unexpectedly erupted, exposing our false securities. Aside from the different ways that various countries responded to the crisis, their inability to work together became quite evident. For all our hyper-connectivity, we witnessed a fragmentation that made it more difficult to resolve problems that affect us all. Anyone who thinks that the only lesson to be learned was the need to improve what we were already doing, or to refine existing systems and regulations, is denying reality.

8. It is my desire that, in this our time, by acknowledging the dignity of each human person, we can contribute to the rebirth of a universal aspiration to fraternity. Brotherhood between all men and women. "Here we have a splendid secret that shows us how to dream and to turn our life into a wonderful adventure. No one can face life in isolation... We need a community that supports and helps us, in which we can help one another to keep looking ahead. How important it is to dream together... By ourselves, we risk seeing mirages, things that are not there. Dreams, on the other hand, are built together."[6] Let us dream, then, as a single human family, as fellow travelers sharing the same flesh, as children of the same earth which is our common home, each of us bringing the richness of his or her beliefs and convictions, each of us with his or her own voice, brothers and sisters all.

> "Let us dream, then as a single human family, as fellow travelers sharing the same flesh, as children of the

6. *Address at the Ecumenical and Interreligious Meeting with Young People*, Skopje, North Macedonia (7 May 2019): *L'Osservatore Romano*, 9 May 2019, p. 9.

same earth which is our common home, each of us bringing the richness of his or her beliefs and convictions, each of us with his or her own voice, brothers and sisters all" (no. 8).

QUESTIONS FOR REFLECTION AND DISCUSSION

1. What hopes and expectations do you bring to this encyclical—and why?
2. What reservations or concerns do you bring to this encyclical—and why?
3. How can you open yourself to the presence and power of the Holy Spirit so reading this encyclical can be an illuminating, encouraging, and challenging experience in your faith journey?

FOR FURTHER READING

Brackley, Dean. *The Call to Discernment in Troubled Times.* New York: Crossroad, 2004.

Markey, John J. *Moses in Pharaoh's House: A Liberation Spirituality for North America.* Winona, MN: Anselm Academic, 2014.

Vasko, Elisabeth T. *Beyond Apathy: A Theology for Bystanders.* Minneapolis: Fortress Press, 2015.

Chapter One

DARK CLOUDS OVER A CLOSED WORLD

SYNOPSIS

Pope Francis dedicates the first chapter of *Fratelli Tutti* to a sobering look at the "signs of the times" (Matt 16:3). Although it is not an exhaustive overview of human experience, this section of the encyclical points to the beliefs and practices that betray human dignity and undermine our ability to encounter and engage one another in equal respect and reciprocal concern. Solidarity is impossible if we cannot share life together, if some are deprived the fullness of God's love intended for all (Eph 3:17–19). For this reason, Pope Francis draws our attention to the "shattered dreams" caused by "reductive anthropological visions" that allow injustice to persist (no. 22). His goal is not to fan the flames of a culture war or cast the church as a perfect society in contrast to a sinful world. Instead, this first chapter invites the reader to pay attention to the social norms, political and economic systems, as well as the structures marked by vice and sin. Cultures are created by patterns of human beliefs, values, and actions; just as individual behavior helps construct culture, so cultural mores influence personal opinions, morals, and conduct. Chapter 1 investigates how human free will is shaping culture and the impact these cultures have on moral identity, agency, and relationships. Our task is to better understand whether and how our relationship with our wider society is helping or hindering the promotion of truth, freedom, respect, compassion, cooperation, love, justice, solidarity, and peace. Just as we have to ward against, repent, and atone for personal sin, we also have to be on guard so as to avoid participating in—or benefitting from—social sins and sinful structures.

The first chapter of *Fratelli Tutti* provides a template for practicing the first and second steps in the pastoral spiral. First, insertion takes heed of our social location, since what we see depends on where—and with whom—we stand. Pope Francis laments that "we are more alone than ever," especially when taking up the perspective of those excluded and exploited by the powerful (no. 12). From the vantage point of the margins, we can see the harmful effects of a "certain regression" that ignores or rejects lessons from history, including the return of "extremist, resentful and aggressive nationalism" (no. 11). Pope Francis underscores the experience of women as disproportionately susceptible to discrimination and exclusion as well as abuse and violence (no. 23). We also see the costs of progress without a shared commitment to the common good: tremendous technological advances make life more convenient and efficient for many, while millions of children continue to die from poverty and hunger (no. 29).

COVID-19 both caused and exposed a great deal of social distrust and division. The second step of the pastoral spiral is dedicated to the social analysis of the root causes of these beliefs and practices. The pandemic and a host of natural disasters lift up the cry of those who are most vulnerable (no. 34). Most of us have had to deal with displacement from our usual roles and routines but have not endured the duress and desperation that force people to flee their homes, exacerbating crises along national borders. Pope Francis critiques ideologies that fear difference, fuel disillusionment, sew suspicion and scorn, or endorse a "globalized indifference" at the suffering of our neighbors (nos. 13, 30). He warns against the "temptation to build a culture of walls," since "those who raise walls will end up slaves within the very walls they have built" (no. 27). Pope Francis compares the fear and alarm shown to migrants and refugees with the repeated command in Scripture to welcome the stranger (Deut 10:19; Lev 19:34; Jer 7:5–7; Matt 25:35; Rom 12:13; Col 3:11; Heb 13:1–3), urging us to resist the xenophobia and racism that "deprive us of the desire and the ability to encounter the other" (no. 41).

In a new development for the canon of Catholic social teaching, Pope Francis also devotes several paragraphs to the effects of digital technology and social networks (nos. 42–50). The loss of privacy, rapid spread of disinformation, rise of aggression and slander, and habits of instant gratification jeopardize access to the truth, opportunities to be reflective, and respectful engagement with others. Even though these tools wield unprecedented avenues for connection, online echo chambers make it harder to cultivate empathy and understanding across differences, deepening divides. Screens make it easier to objectify others, hide behind anonymity, and imperil healthy self-esteem. Pope Francis's concerns about these digital tools are verified by social science research showing that the more time people spend with social media, the higher their feelings of anxiety, depression, and social isolation.

These are not comfortable perspectives to make our own. But this first chapter reminds us that we cannot ignore "that the whole creation has been groaning in labor pains"

(Rom 8:22). These are problems too big for kindness or tolerance to solve. As we listen to this cry for life and lamentation of communities in crisis, God calls us to be sources of comfort and strength for those who suffer. And God enables us to be coworkers (1 Cor 3:9) for a world made whole. But to accomplish this, we have to disrupt the status quo where "the sense of belonging to a single human family is fading" in a "world that races ahead, yet lacks a shared roadmap" (nos. 30–31). Profit or progress cannot be the bottom line, especially if they are not put in service of the common good. To inspire a commitment to create change, Pope Francis concludes this section with two paragraphs focusing on reasons for hope. This encyclical serves as a graced moment to recognize our "thirst, an aspiration, a longing for a life of fulfillment, a desire to achieve great things" (no. 55). If we turn our hearts to God and dream boldly together, we can stretch our vision to new horizons of possibility for ourselves and for each other.

---

9. Without claiming to carry out an exhaustive analysis or to study every aspect of our present-day experience, I intend simply to consider certain trends in our world that hinder the development of universal fraternity.

SHATTERED DREAMS

10. For decades, it seemed that the world had learned a lesson from its many wars and disasters, and was slowly moving towards various forms of integration. For example, there was the dream of a united Europe, capable of acknowledging its shared roots and rejoicing in its rich diversity. We think of "the firm conviction of the founders of the European Union, who envisioned a future based on the capacity to work together in bridging divisions and in fostering peace and fellowship between all the peoples of

this continent."[7] There was also a growing desire for integration in Latin America, and several steps were taken in this direction. In some countries and regions, attempts at reconciliation and rapprochement proved fruitful, while others showed great promise.

11. Our own days, however, seem to be showing signs of a certain regression. Ancient conflicts thought long buried are breaking out anew, while instances of a myopic, extremist, resentful and aggressive nationalism are on the rise. In some countries, a concept of popular and national unity influenced by various ideologies is creating new forms of selfishness and a loss of the social sense under the guise of defending national interests. Once more we are being reminded that "each new generation must take up the struggles and attainments of past generations, while setting its sights even higher. This is the path. Goodness, together with love, justice and solidarity, are not achieved once and for all; they have to be realized each day. It is not possible to settle for what was achieved in the past and complacently enjoy it, as if we could somehow disregard the fact that many of our brothers and sisters still endure situations that cry out for our attention."[8]

12. "Opening up to the world" is an expression that has been co-opted by the economic and financial sector and is now used exclusively of openness to foreign interests or to the freedom of economic powers to invest without obstacles or complications in all countries. Local conflicts and disregard for the common good are exploited by the global economy in order to impose a single cultural model. This culture unifies the world, but divides persons and nations, for "as society becomes ever more globalized, it makes us neighbours, but does not make us brothers."[9] We are more alone than ever in an increasingly massified world that promotes individual interests and weakens the communitarian dimension of life. Indeed, there are markets where individuals

---

7. *Address to the European Parliament*, Strasbourg (25 November 2014): AAS 106 (2014), 996.

8. *Meeting with Authorities, Civil Society and the Diplomatic Corps*, Santiago, Chile (16 January 2018): AAS 110 (2018), 256.

9. Benedict XVI, Encyclical Letter *Caritas in Veritate* (29 June 2009), 19: AAS 101 (2009), 655.

become mere consumers or bystanders. As a rule, the advance of this kind of globalism strengthens the identity of the more powerful, who can protect themselves, but it tends to diminish the identity of the weaker and poorer regions, making them more vulnerable and dependent. In this way, political life becomes increasingly fragile in the face of transnational economic powers that operate with the principle of "divide and conquer."

> "We are more alone than ever in an increasingly massified world that promotes individual interests and weakens the communitarian dimension of life. Indeed, there are markets where individuals become mere consumers or bystanders. As a rule, the advance of this kind of globalism strengthens the identity of the more powerful, who can protect themselves, but it tends to diminish the identity of the weaker and poorer regions, making them more vulnerable and dependent" (no 12).

The end of historical consciousness

13. As a result, there is a growing loss of the sense of history, which leads to even further breakup. A kind of "deconstructionism," whereby human freedom claims to create everything starting from zero, is making headway in today's culture. The one thing it leaves in its wake is the drive to limitless consumption and expressions of empty individualism. Concern about this led me to offer the young some advice. "If someone tells young people to ignore their history, to reject the experiences of their elders, to look down on the past and to look forward to a future that he himself holds out, doesn't it then become easy to draw them along so that they only do what he tells them? He needs the young to be shallow, uprooted and distrustful, so that they can trust only in his promises and act according to his plans. That is how various ideologies operate: they destroy (or deconstruct) all differences so that they can reign unopposed. To do so, however,

they need young people who have no use for history, who spurn the spiritual and human riches inherited from past generations, and are ignorant of everything that came before them."[10]

14. These are the new forms of cultural colonization. Let us not forget that "peoples that abandon their tradition and, either from a craze to mimic others or to foment violence, or from unpardonable negligence or apathy, allow others to rob their very soul, end up losing not only their spiritual identity but also their moral consistency and, in the end, their intellectual, economic and political independence."[11] One effective way to weaken historical consciousness, critical thinking, the struggle for justice and the processes of integration is to empty great words of their meaning or to manipulate them. Nowadays, what do certain words like democracy, freedom, justice or unity really mean? They have been bent and shaped to serve as tools for domination, as meaningless tags that can be used to justify any action.

LACKING A PLAN FOR EVERYONE

15. The best way to dominate and gain control over people is to spread despair and discouragement, even under the guise of defending certain values. Today, in many countries, hyperbole, extremism and polarization have become political tools. Employing a strategy of ridicule, suspicion and relentless criticism, in a variety of ways one denies the right of others to exist or to have an opinion. Their share of the truth and their values are rejected and, as a result, the life of society is impoverished and subjected to the hubris of the powerful. Political life no longer has to do with healthy debates about long-term plans to improve people's lives and to advance the common good, but only with slick marketing techniques primarily aimed at discrediting others. In this craven

10. Post-Synodal Apostolic Exhortation *Christus Vivit* (25 March 2019), 181.

11. Cardinal Raúl Silva Henríquez, *Homily at the Te Deum*, Santiago de Chile (18 September 1974).

exchange of charges and counter-charges, debate degenerates into a permanent state of disagreement and confrontation.

16. Amid the fray of conflicting interests, where victory consists in eliminating one's opponents, how is it possible to raise our sights to recognize our neighbours or to help those who have fallen along the way? A plan that would set great goals for the development of our entire human family nowadays sounds like madness. We are growing ever more distant from one another, while the slow and demanding march towards an increasingly united and just world is suffering a new and dramatic setback.

17. To care for the world in which we live means to care for ourselves. Yet we need to think of ourselves more and more as a single family dwelling in a common home. Such care does not interest those economic powers that demand quick profits. Often the voices raised in defence of the environment are silenced or ridiculed, using apparently reasonable arguments that are merely a screen for special interests. In this shallow, short-sighted culture that we have created, bereft of a shared vision, "it is foreseeable that, once certain resources have been depleted, the scene will be set for new wars, albeit under the guise of noble claims."[12]

A "throwaway" world

18. Some parts of our human family, it appears, can be readily sacrificed for the sake of others considered worthy of a carefree existence. Ultimately, "persons are no longer seen as a paramount value to be cared for and respected, especially when they are poor and disabled, 'not yet useful'—like the unborn, or 'no longer needed'—like the elderly. We have grown indifferent to all kinds of wastefulness, starting with the waste of food, which is deplorable in the extreme."[13]

19. A decline in the birthrate, which leads to the aging of the population, together with the relegation of the elderly to a

12. Encyclical Letter *Laudato Si'* (24 May 2015), 57: AAS 107 (2015), 869.

13. *Address to the Diplomatic Corps accredited to the Holy See* (11 January 2016): AAS 108 (2016), 120.

sad and lonely existence, is a subtle way of stating that it is all about us, that our individual concerns are the only thing that matters. In this way, "what is thrown away are not only food and dispensable objects, but often human beings themselves."[14] We have seen what happened with the elderly in certain places in our world as a result of the coronavirus. They did not have to die that way. Yet something similar had long been occurring during heat waves and in other situations: older people found themselves cruelly abandoned. We fail to realize that, by isolating the elderly and leaving them in the care of others without the closeness and concern of family members, we disfigure and impoverish the family itself. We also end up depriving young people of a necessary connection to their roots and a wisdom that the young cannot achieve on their own.

20. This way of discarding others can take a variety of forms, such as an obsession with reducing labour costs with no concern for its grave consequences, since the unemployment that it directly generates leads to the expansion of poverty.[15] In addition, a readiness to discard others finds expression in vicious attitudes that we thought long past, such as racism, which retreats underground only to keep reemerging. Instances of racism continue to shame us, for they show that our supposed social progress is not as real or definitive as we think.

"A readiness to discard others finds expression in vicious attitudes that we thought long past, such as racism, which retreats underground only to keep reemerging. Instances of racism continue to shame us, for they show that our supposed social progress is not as real or definitive as we think" (no. 20).

14. *Address to the Diplomatic Corps accredited to the Holy See* (13 January 2014): AAS 106 (2014), 83–84.

15. Cf. *Address to the "Centesimus Annus pro Pontifice" Foundation* (25 May 2013): *Insegnamenti* I, 1 (2013), 238.

21. Some economic rules have proved effective for growth, but not for integral human development.[16] Wealth has increased, but together with inequality, with the result that "new forms of poverty are emerging."[17] The claim that the modern world has reduced poverty is made by measuring poverty with criteria from the past that do not correspond to present-day realities. In other times, for example, lack of access to electric energy was not considered a sign of poverty, nor was it a source of hardship. Poverty must always be understood and gauged in the context of the actual opportunities available in each concrete historical period.

Insufficiently universal human rights

22. It frequently becomes clear that, in practice, human rights are not equal for all. Respect for those rights "is the preliminary condition for a country's social and economic development. When the dignity of the human person is respected, and his or her rights recognized and guaranteed, creativity and interdependence thrive, and the creativity of the human personality is released through actions that further the common good."[18] Yet, "by closely observing our contemporary societies, we see numerous contradictions that lead us to wonder whether the equal dignity of all human beings, solemnly proclaimed seventy years ago, is truly recognized, respected, protected and promoted in every situation. In today's world, many forms of injustice persist, fed by reductive anthropological visions and by a profit-based economic model that does not hesitate to exploit, discard and even kill human beings. While one part of humanity lives in opulence, another part sees its own dignity denied, scorned or trampled upon, and its fundamental rights discarded or violated."[19] What

16. Cf. Saint Paul VI, Encyclical Letter *Populorum Progressio* (26 March 1967): AAS 59 (1967), 264.

17. Benedict XVI, Encyclical Letter *Caritas in Veritate* (29 June 2009), 22: AAS 101 (2009), 657.

18. *Address to the Civil Authorities*, Tirana, Albania (21 September 2014): AAS 106 (2014), 773.

19. *Message to Participants in the International Conference "Human Rights in*

does this tell us about the equality of rights grounded in innate human dignity?

23. Similarly, the organization of societies worldwide is still far from reflecting clearly that women possess the same dignity and identical rights as men. We say one thing with words, but our decisions and reality tell another story. Indeed, "doubly poor are those women who endure situations of exclusion, mistreatment and violence, since they are frequently less able to defend their rights."[20]

> "The organization of societies worldwide is still far from reflecting clearly that women possess the same dignity and identical rights as men. We say one thing with words, but our decisions and reality tell another story" (no. 23).

24. We should also recognize that "even though the international community has adopted numerous agreements aimed at ending slavery in all its forms, and has launched various strategies to combat this phenomenon, millions of people today—children, women and men of all ages—are deprived of freedom and forced to live in conditions akin to slavery… Today, as in the past, slavery is rooted in a notion of the human person that allows him or her to be treated as an object… Whether by coercion, or deception, or by physical or psychological duress, human persons created in the image and likeness of God are deprived of their freedom, sold and reduced to being the property of others. They are treated as means to an end… [Criminal networks] are skilled in using modern means of communication as a way of luring young men and women in various parts of the world."[21] A perversion that exceeds

the Contemporary World: Achievements, Omissions, Negations" (10 December 2018): *L'Osservatore Romano*, 10–11 December 2018, p. 8.

20. Apostolic Exhortation *Evangelii Gaudium* (24 November 2013), 212: AAS 105 (2013), 1108.

21. *Message for the 2015 World Day of Peace* (8 December 2014), 3–4: AAS 107 (2015), 69–71.

all limits when it subjugates women and then forces them to abort. An abomination that goes to the length of kidnapping persons for the sake of selling their organs. Trafficking in persons and other contemporary forms of enslavement are a worldwide problem that needs to be taken seriously by humanity as a whole: "since criminal organizations employ global networks to achieve their goals, efforts to eliminate this phenomenon also demand a common and, indeed, a global effort on the part of various sectors of society."[22]

Conflict and fear

25. War, terrorist attacks, racial or religious persecution, and many other affronts to human dignity are judged differently, depending on how convenient it proves for certain, primarily economic, interests. What is true as long as it is convenient for someone in power stops being true once it becomes inconvenient. These situations of violence, sad to say, "have become so common as to constitute a real 'third world war' fought piecemeal."[23]

26. This should not be surprising, if we realize that we no longer have common horizons that unite us; indeed, the first victim of every war is "the human family's innate vocation to brotherhood." As a result, "every threatening situation breeds mistrust and leads people to withdraw into their own safety zone."[24] Our world is trapped in a strange contradiction: we believe that we can "ensure stability and peace through a false sense of security sustained by a mentality of fear and mistrust."[25]

27. Paradoxically, we have certain ancestral fears that technological development has not succeeded in eliminating; indeed, those fears have been able to hide and spread behind

22. Ibid., 5: AAS 107 (2015), 72.

23. *Message for the 2016 World Day of Peace* (8 December 2015), 2: AAS 108 (2016), 49.

24. *Message for the 2020 World Day of Peace* (8 December 2019), 1: *L'Osservatore Romano*, 13 December 2019, p. 8.

25. *Address on Nuclear Weapons*, Nagasaki, Japan (24 November 2019): *L'Osservatore Romano*, 25–26 November 2019, p. 6.

new technologies. Today too, outside the ancient town walls lies the abyss, the territory of the unknown, the wilderness. Whatever comes from there cannot be trusted, for it is unknown, unfamiliar, not part of the village. It is the territory of the "barbarian," from whom we must defend ourselves at all costs. As a result, new walls are erected for self-preservation, the outside world ceases to exist and leaves only "my" world, to the point that others, no longer considered human beings possessed of an inalienable dignity, become only "them." Once more, we encounter "the temptation to build a culture of walls, to raise walls, walls in the heart, walls on the land, in order to prevent this encounter with other cultures, with other people. And those who raise walls will end up as slaves within the very walls they have built. They are left without horizons, for they lack this interchange with others."[26]

28. The loneliness, fear and insecurity experienced by those who feel abandoned by the system creates a fertile terrain for various "mafias." These flourish because they claim to be defenders of the forgotten, often by providing various forms of assistance even as they pursue their criminal interests. There also exists a typically "mafioso" pedagogy that, by appealing to a false communitarian mystique, creates bonds of dependency and fealty from which it is very difficult to break free.

GLOBALIZATION AND PROGRESS WITHOUT A SHARED ROADMAP

29. With the Grand Imam Ahmad Al-Tayyeb, we do not ignore the positive advances made in the areas of science, technology, medicine, industry and welfare, above all in developed countries. Nonetheless, "we wish to emphasize that, together with these historical advances, great and valued as they are, there exists a moral deterioration that influences international

26. *Dialogue with Students and Teachers of the San Carlo College in Milan* (6 April 2019): *L'Osservatore Romano*, 8–9 April 2019, p. 6.

action and a weakening of spiritual values and responsibility. This contributes to a general feeling of frustration, isolation and desperation." We see "outbreaks of tension and a buildup of arms and ammunition in a global context dominated by uncertainty, disillusionment, fear of the future, and controlled by narrow economic interests." We can also point to "major political crises, situations of injustice and the lack of an equitable distribution of natural resources... In the face of such crises that result in the deaths of millions of children—emaciated from poverty and hunger—there is an unacceptable silence on the international level."[27] This panorama, for all its undeniable advances, does not appear to lead to a more humane future.

30. In today's world, the sense of belonging to a single human family is fading, and the dream of working together for justice and peace seems an outdated utopia. What reigns instead is a cool, comfortable and globalized indifference, born of deep disillusionment concealed behind a deceptive illusion: thinking that we are all-powerful, while failing to realize that we are all in the same boat. This illusion, unmindful of the great fraternal values, leads to "a sort of cynicism. For that is the temptation we face if we go down the road of disenchantment and disappointment... Isolation and withdrawal into one's own interests are never the way to restore hope and bring about renewal. Rather, it is closeness; it is the culture of encounter. Isolation, no; closeness, yes. Culture clash, no; culture of encounter, yes."[28]

31. In this world that races ahead, yet lacks a shared roadmap, we increasingly sense that "the gap between concern for one's personal well-being and the prosperity of the larger human family seems to be stretching to the point of complete division between individuals and human community... It is one thing to feel forced to live together, but something entirely different to value the richness and beauty of those seeds of common life that

---

27. *Document on Human Fraternity for World Peace and Living Together*, Abu Dhabi (4 February 2019): *L'Osservatore Romano*, 4–5 February 2019, p. 6.

28. *Address to the World of Culture*, Cagliari, Italy (22 September 2013): *L'Osservatore Romano*, 23–24 September 2013, p. 7.

need to be sought out and cultivated."[29] Technology is constantly advancing, yet "how wonderful it would be if the growth of scientific and technological innovation could come with more equality and social inclusion. How wonderful would it be, even as we discover faraway planets, to rediscover the needs of the brothers and sisters who orbit around us."[30]

PANDEMICS AND OTHER CALAMITIES IN HISTORY

32. True, a worldwide tragedy like the Covid-19 pandemic momentarily revived the sense that we are a global community, all in the same boat, where one person's problems are the problems of all. Once more we realized that no one is saved alone; we can only be saved together. As I said in those days, "the storm has exposed our vulnerability and uncovered those false and superfluous certainties around which we constructed our daily schedules, our projects, our habits and priorities… Amid this storm, the façade of those stereotypes with which we camouflaged our egos, always worrying about appearances, has fallen away, revealing once more the ineluctable and blessed awareness that we are part of one another, that we are brothers and sisters of one another."[31]

> "A worldwide tragedy like the Covid-19 pandemic momentarily revived the sense that we are a global community, all in the same boat, where one person's

29. *Humana Communitas.* Letter to the President of the Pontifical Academy for Life on the Twenty-fifth Anniversary of Its Founding (6 January 2019), 2.6: *L'Osservatore Romano*, 16 January 2019, pp. 6–7.

30. *Video Message to the TED Conference in Vancouver* (26 April 2017): *L'Osservatore Romano*, 27 April 2017, p. 7.

31. *Extraordinary Moment of Prayer in Time of Epidemic* (27 March 2020): *L'Osservatore Romano*, 29 March 2020, p. 10.

problems are the problems of all. Once more we realized that no one is saved alone; we can only be saved together" (no. 32).

33. The world was relentlessly moving towards an economy that, thanks to technological progress, sought to reduce "human costs"; there were those who would have had us believe that freedom of the market was sufficient to keep everything secure. Yet the brutal and unforeseen blow of this uncontrolled pandemic forced us to recover our concern for human beings, for everyone, rather than for the benefit of a few. Today we can recognize that "we fed ourselves on dreams of splendour and grandeur, and ended up consuming distraction, insularity and solitude. We gorged ourselves on networking, and lost the taste of fraternity. We looked for quick and safe results, only to find ourselves overwhelmed by impatience and anxiety. Prisoners of a virtual reality, we lost the taste and flavour of the truly real."[32] The pain, uncertainty and fear, and the realization of our own limitations, brought on by the pandemic have only made it all the more urgent that we rethink our styles of life, our relationships, the organization of our societies and, above all, the meaning of our existence.

34. If everything is connected, it is hard to imagine that this global disaster is unrelated to our way of approaching reality, our claim to be absolute masters of our own lives and of all that exists. I do not want to speak of divine retribution, nor would it be sufficient to say that the harm we do to nature is itself the punishment for our offences. The world is itself crying out in rebellion. We are reminded of the well-known verse of the poet Virgil that evokes the "tears of things," the misfortunes of life and history.[33]

35. All too quickly, however, we forget the lessons of history, "the teacher of life."[34] Once this health crisis passes, our worst

32. *Homily* in Skopje, North Macedonia (7 May 2019): *L'Osservatore Romano*, 8 May 2019, p. 12.

33. Cf. *Aeneid* 1, 462: "*Sunt lacrimae rerum et mentem mortalia tangent.*"

34. "*Historia... magistra vitae*" (Cicero, *De Oratore*, 2, 6).

response would be to plunge even more deeply into feverish consumerism and new forms of egotistic self-preservation. God willing, after all this, we will think no longer in terms of "them" and "those," but only "us." If only this may prove not to be just another tragedy of history from which we learned nothing. If only we might keep in mind all those elderly persons who died for lack of respirators, partly as a result of the dismantling, year after year, of healthcare systems. If only this immense sorrow may not prove useless, but enable us to take a step forward towards a new style of life. If only we might rediscover once for all that we need one another, and that in this way our human family can experience a rebirth, with all its faces, all its hands and all its voices, beyond the walls that we have erected.

36. Unless we recover the shared passion to create a community of belonging and solidarity worthy of our time, our energy and our resources, the global illusion that misled us will collapse and leave many in the grip of anguish and emptiness. Nor should we naively refuse to recognize that "obsession with a consumerist lifestyle, above all when few people are capable of maintaining it, can only lead to violence and mutual destruction."[35] The notion of "every man for himself" will rapidly degenerate into a free-for-all that would prove worse than any pandemic.

AN ABSENCE OF HUMAN DIGNITY ON THE BORDERS

37. Certain populist political regimes, as well as certain liberal economic approaches, maintain that an influx of migrants is to be prevented at all costs. Arguments are also made for the propriety of limiting aid to poor countries, so that they can hit rock bottom and find themselves forced to take austerity measures. One fails to realize that behind such statements, abstract and hard to support, great numbers of lives are at stake. Many

35. Encyclical Letter *Laudato Si'* (24 May 2015), 204: AAS 107 (2015), 928.

migrants have fled from war, persecution and natural catastrophes. Others, rightly, "are seeking opportunities for themselves and their families. They dream of a better future and they want to create the conditions for achieving it."[36]

38. Sadly, some "are attracted by Western culture, sometimes with unrealistic expectations that expose them to grave disappointments. Unscrupulous traffickers, frequently linked to drug cartels or arms cartels, exploit the weakness of migrants, who too often experience violence, trafficking, psychological and physical abuse and untold sufferings on their journey."[37] Those who emigrate "experience separation from their place of origin, and often a cultural and religious uprooting as well. Fragmentation is also felt by the communities they leave behind, which lose their most vigorous and enterprising elements, and by families, especially when one or both of the parents migrates, leaving the children in the country of origin."[38] For this reason, "there is also a need to reaffirm the right not to emigrate, that is, to remain in one's homeland."[39]

39. Then too, "in some host countries, migration causes fear and alarm, often fomented and exploited for political purposes. This can lead to a xenophobic mentality, as people close in on themselves, and it needs to be addressed decisively."[40] Migrants are not seen as entitled like others to participate in the life of society, and it is forgotten that they possess the same intrinsic dignity as any person. Hence they ought to be "agents in their own redemption."[41] No one will ever openly deny that they are human beings, yet in practice, by our decisions and the way we treat them, we can show that we consider them less worthy, less important, less human. For Christians, this way of thinking and acting is unacceptable, since it sets certain political preferences

---

36. Post-Synodal Apostolic Exhortation *Christus Vivit* (25 March 2019), 91.

37. Ibid., 92.

38. Ibid., 93.

39. Benedict XVI, *Message for the 2013 World Day of Migrants and Refugees* (12 October 2012): AAS 104 (2012), 908.

40. Post-Synodal Apostolic Exhortation *Christus Vivit* (25 March 2019), 92.

41. *Message for the 2020 World Day of Migrants and Refugees* (13 May 2020): *L'Osservatore Romano*, 16 May 2020, p. 8.

above deep convictions of our faith: the inalienable dignity of each human person regardless of origin, race or religion, and the supreme law of fraternal love.

40. "Migrations, more than ever before, will play a pivotal role in the future of our world."[42] At present, however, migration is affected by the "loss of that sense of responsibility for our brothers and sisters on which every civil society is based."[43] Europe, for example, seriously risks taking this path. Nonetheless, "aided by its great cultural and religious heritage, it has the means to defend the centrality of the human person and to find the right balance between its twofold moral responsibility to protect the rights of its citizens and to assure assistance and acceptance to migrants."[44]

41. I realize that some people are hesitant and fearful with regard to migrants. I consider this part of our natural instinct of self-defence. Yet it is also true that an individual and a people are only fruitful and productive if they are able to develop a creative openness to others. I ask everyone to move beyond those primal reactions because "there is a problem when doubts and fears condition our way of thinking and acting to the point of making us intolerant, closed and perhaps even—without realizing it—racist. In this way, fear deprives us of the desire and the ability to encounter the other."[45]

THE ILLUSION OF COMMUNICATION

42. Oddly enough, while closed and intolerant attitudes towards others are on the rise, distances are otherwise shrinking or

---

42. *Address to the Diplomatic Corps accredited to the Holy See* (11 January 2016): AAS 108 (2016), 124.

43. *Address to the Diplomatic Corps accredited to the Holy See* (13 January 2014): AAS 106 (2014), 84.

44. *Address to the Diplomatic Corps accredited to the Holy See* (11 January 2016): AAS 108 (2016), 123.

45. *Message for the 2019 World Day of Migrants and Refugees* (27 May 2019): *L'Osservatore Romano*, 27–28 May 2019, p. 8.

disappearing to the point that the right to privacy scarcely exists. Everything has become a kind of spectacle to be examined and inspected, and people's lives are now under constant surveillance. Digital communication wants to bring everything out into the open; people's lives are combed over, laid bare and bandied about, often anonymously. Respect for others disintegrates, and even as we dismiss, ignore or keep others distant, we can shamelessly peer into every detail of their lives.

43. Digital campaigns of hatred and destruction, for their part, are not—as some would have us believe—a positive form of mutual support, but simply an association of individuals united against a perceived common enemy. "Digital media can also expose people to the risk of addiction, isolation and a gradual loss of contact with concrete reality, blocking the development of authentic interpersonal relationships."[46] They lack the physical gestures, facial expressions, moments of silence, body language and even the smells, the trembling of hands, the blushes and perspiration that speak to us and are a part of human communication. Digital relationships, which do not demand the slow and gradual cultivation of friendships, stable interaction or the building of a consensus that matures over time, have the appearance of sociability. Yet they do not really build community; instead, they tend to disguise and expand the very individualism that finds expression in xenophobia and in contempt for the vulnerable. Digital connectivity is not enough to build bridges. It is not capable of uniting humanity.

Shameless aggression

44. Even as individuals maintain their comfortable consumerist isolation, they can choose a form of constant and febrile bonding that encourages remarkable hostility, insults, abuse, defamation and verbal violence destructive of others, and this with a lack of restraint that could not exist in physical contact

46. Post-Synodal Apostolic Exhortation *Christus Vivit* (25 March 2019), 88.

without tearing us all apart. Social aggression has found unparalleled room for expansion through computers and mobile devices.

45. This has now given free rein to ideologies. Things that until a few years ago could not be said by anyone without risking the loss of universal respect can now be said with impunity, and in the crudest of terms, even by some political figures. Nor should we forget that "there are huge economic interests operating in the digital world, capable of exercising forms of control as subtle as they are invasive, creating mechanisms for the manipulation of consciences and of the democratic process. The way many platforms work often ends up favouring encounter between persons who think alike, shielding them from debate. These closed circuits facilitate the spread of fake news and false information, fomenting prejudice and hate."[47]

46. We should also recognize that destructive forms of fanaticism are at times found among religious believers, including Christians; they too "can be caught up in networks of verbal violence through the internet and the various forums of digital communication. Even in Catholic media, limits can be overstepped, defamation and slander can become commonplace, and all ethical standards and respect for the good name of others can be abandoned."[48] How can this contribute to the fraternity that our common Father asks of us?

Information without wisdom

47. True wisdom demands an encounter with reality. Today, however, everything can be created, disguised and altered. A direct encounter even with the fringes of reality can thus prove intolerable. A mechanism of selection then comes into play, whereby I can immediately separate likes from dislikes, what I consider attractive from what I deem distasteful. In the same way, we can choose the people with whom we wish to share our world. Persons or situations we find unpleasant or disagreeable are simply deleted in

47. Ibid., 89.

48. Apostolic Exhortation *Gaudete et Exsultate* (19 March 2018), 115.

today's virtual networks; a virtual circle is then created, isolating us from the real world in which we are living.

> "True wisdom demands an encounter with reality. Today, however, everything can be created, disguised and altered. A direct encounter even with the fringes of reality can thus prove intolerable. A mechanism of selection then comes into play, whereby I can immediately separate likes from dislikes, what I consider attractive from what I deem distasteful.... A new lifestyle is emerging, where we create only what we want and exclude all that we cannot control or know instantly and superficially. This process, by its intrinsic logic, blocks the kind of serene reflection that could lead us to a shared wisdom" (nos. 47, 49).

48. The ability to sit down and listen to others, typical of interpersonal encounters, is paradigmatic of the welcoming attitude shown by those who transcend narcissism and accept others, caring for them and welcoming them into their lives. Yet "today's world is largely a deaf world... At times, the frantic pace of the modern world prevents us from listening attentively to what another person is saying. Halfway through, we interrupt him and want to contradict what he has not even finished saying. We must not lose our ability to listen." Saint Francis "heard the voice of God, he heard the voice of the poor, he heard the voice of the infirm and he heard the voice of nature. He made of them a way of life. My desire is that the seed that Saint Francis planted may grow in the hearts of many."[49]

49. As silence and careful listening disappear, replaced by a frenzy of texting, this basic structure of sage human communication is at risk. A new lifestyle is emerging, where we create only what we want and exclude all that we cannot control or know

49. From the film *Pope Francis: A Man of His Word*, by Wim Wenders (2018).

instantly and superficially. This process, by its intrinsic logic, blocks the kind of serene reflection that could lead us to a shared wisdom.

50. Together, we can seek the truth in dialogue, in relaxed conversation or in passionate debate. To do so calls for perseverance; it entails moments of silence and suffering, yet it can patiently embrace the broader experience of individuals and peoples. The flood of information at our fingertips does not make for greater wisdom. Wisdom is not born of quick searches on the internet nor is it a mass of unverified data. That is not the way to mature in the encounter with truth. Conversations revolve only around the latest data; they become merely horizontal and cumulative. We fail to keep our attention focused, to penetrate to the heart of matters, and to recognize what is essential to give meaning to our lives. Freedom thus becomes an illusion that we are peddled, easily confused with the ability to navigate the internet. The process of building fraternity, be it local or universal, can only be undertaken by spirits that are free and open to authentic encounters.

FORMS OF SUBJECTION AND OF SELF-CONTEMPT

51. Certain economically prosperous countries tend to be proposed as cultural models for less developed countries; instead, each of those countries should be helped to grow in its own distinct way and to develop its capacity for innovation while respecting the values of its proper culture. A shallow and pathetic desire to imitate others leads to copying and consuming in place of creating, and fosters low national self-esteem. In the affluent sectors of many poor countries, and at times in those who have recently emerged from poverty, there is a resistance to native ways of thinking and acting, and a tendency to look down on one's own cultural identity, as if it were the sole cause of every ill.

52. Destroying self-esteem is an easy way to dominate others. Behind these trends that tend to level our world, there

flourish powerful interests that take advantage of such low self-esteem, while attempting, through the media and networks, to create a new culture in the service of the elite. This plays into the opportunism of financial speculators and raiders, and the poor always end up the losers. Then too, ignoring the culture of their people has led to the inability of many political leaders to devise an effective development plan that could be freely accepted and sustained over time.

53. We forget that "there is no worse form of alienation than to feel uprooted, belonging to no one. A land will be fruitful, and its people bear fruit and give birth to the future, only to the extent that it can foster a sense of belonging among its members, create bonds of integration between generations and different communities, and avoid all that makes us insensitive to others and leads to further alienation."[50]

HOPE

54. Despite these dark clouds, which may not be ignored, I would like in the following pages to take up and discuss many new paths of hope. For God continues to sow abundant seeds of goodness in our human family. The recent pandemic enabled us to recognize and appreciate once more all those around us who, in the midst of fear, responded by putting their lives on the line. We began to realize that our lives are interwoven with and sustained by ordinary people valiantly shaping the decisive events of our shared history: doctors, nurses, pharmacists, storekeepers and supermarket workers, cleaning personnel, caretakers, transport workers, men and women working to provide essential services and public safety, volunteers, priests and religious... They understood that no one is saved alone.[51]

---

50. *Address to Authorities, Civil Society and the Diplomatic Corps*, Tallinn, Estonia (25 September 2018): *L'Osservatore Romano*, 27 September 2018, p. 7.

51. Cf. *Extraordinary Moment of Prayer in Time of Epidemic* (27 March 2020): *L'Osservatore Romano*, 29 March 2020, p. 10.

55. I invite everyone to renewed hope, for hope "speaks to us of something deeply rooted in every human heart, independently of our circumstances and historical conditioning. Hope speaks to us of a thirst, an aspiration, a longing for a life of fulfillment, a desire to achieve great things, things that fill our heart and lift our spirit to lofty realities like truth, goodness and beauty, justice and love... Hope is bold; it can look beyond personal convenience, the petty securities and compensations which limit our horizon, and it can open us up to grand ideals that make life more beautiful and worthwhile."[52] Let us continue, then, to advance along the paths of hope.

QUESTIONS FOR REFLECTION AND DISCUSSION

1. Notice your thoughts and feelings as you read through the first chapter. What resonates with you—and why? What doesn't register with your experience—and why? What does this make you wonder or question about the experience of others, especially those on the margins of status, privilege, or power? How does this section of the encyclical invite you to consider how others are impacted by the choices you make?
2. Paragraphs 18–21 repeat Pope Francis's critique of "throw-away culture" from his 2015 encyclical, *Laudato Si'* (see, e.g., nos. 16, 22, 43). How does this affect people's lives? What has to change to overcome the "comfortable and globalized indifference" that keeps us from realizing "we are all in the same boat" (no. 30)? What does this require of you and your religious community, especially in confronting the marginalization of women (no. 23)?

52. *Greeting to Young People at the Padre Félix Varela Cultural Centre*, Havana, Cuba (20 September 2015): *L'Osservatore Romano*, 21–22 September 2015, p. 6.

3. Although many individuals experience social isolation and discrimination, *Fratelli Tutti* addresses the particular sin of racism in paragraph 20. How can you practice social analysis to better understand the prevalence and persistence of racism? Racism won't be toppled unless and until we move from being nonracist to antiracist. How can you embrace this opportunity to be more intentional about dismantling racist beliefs, policies, and systems? How can you invite others to join you in these efforts?
4. Pope Francis seems to claim that technology is turning us into contemporary Goldilockses who expect everything catered to our interests, separating us from undesirable content and connections, and buffering us from reality. How does this section of the encyclical challenge you to think about your relationship with your phone, tablet, or computer? The pope contends, "Digital connectivity is not enough to build bridges. It is not capable of uniting humanity" (no. 43). How do you respond—and why? What would it take to use these digital tools and networks for authentic exchange, mutual respect, and inclusive belonging?
5. At the end of the first chapter, Pope Francis appeals to everyone to discover "renewed hope" that is bold, seeking what makes "life more beautiful" (no. 55). What gives you hope—and why? How do you think you are—and can continue to be—a source of hope for others? Where can you look for inspiration that change is possible, and perhaps already in motion?

FOR FURTHER READING

Arbuckle, Gerald A. *Loneliness: Insights for Healing in a Fragmented World*. Maryknoll, NY: Orbis Books, 2018.

Dunson, Donald H., and James A. Dunson III. *Citizen of the World: Suffering and Solidarity in the 21st Century*. Maryknoll, NY: Orbis Books, 2013.

Gebara, Ivone. *Out of the Depths: Women's Experience of Evil and Salvation*. Minneapolis: Fortress, 2002.

Merton, Thomas. *New Seeds of Contemplation*. New York: New Directions, 1961.

Mescher, Marcus. *The Ethics of Encounter: Christian Neighbor Love as a Practice of Solidarity*. Maryknoll, NY: Orbis Books, 2020.

Chapter Two

A STRANGER ON THE ROAD

SYNOPSIS

The second chapter of *Fratelli Tutti* begins the third step of the pastoral spiral: theological reflection. It does so by invoking the passage popularly known as the parable of the Good Samaritan (Luke 10:25–37). This may be Jesus's best-known tale, but it is often domesticated by endorsing random acts of kindness or offering aid in an emergency. As a result, we miss the scope of the challenge to "Go and do likewise."* This section of the encyclical offers us a more detailed look at how God rejects "fatalism as a justification for our own indifference" in the face of suffering and injustice, instead encouraging us "to create a different culture, in which we resolve our conflicts and care for one another" (no. 57). Pope Francis articulates a theology of solidarity informed by numerous biblical verses that oblige us to adopt a posture

* For a robust treatment of this passage and its moral demands, see Marcus Mescher, *The Ethics of Encounter: Christian Neighbor Love as a Practice of Solidarity* (Maryknoll, NY: Orbis Books, 2020), 35–64.

of inclusive love, steadfast compassion, and a preferential commitment to the most vulnerable (no. 61). He urges us to embrace our shared "vocation as citizens of our respective nations and of the entire world, builders of a new social bond" (no. 66). This vocation stems from the Great Commandment to love God and our neighbor as our self.

The details in Luke 10:25–37 help us better understand how Jesus teaches that we love God by loving our neighbor. Here are five key features of the story:

First, it is important to note that Jesus tells this story in response to the question, "What must I do to inherit eternal life?" Although part of a familiar tale to us, this is the most important question a Jewish person could ask. It also means that Jesus's response is more than a suggestion that we practice compassion or generosity; it means that our souls are judged by our commitment to follow the example of the Samaritan.

Second, the lawyer's next question, "Who is my neighbor?" sounds like an innocent clarification but is a limit-seeking question; it seeks to identify the non-neighbors, the ones whom we owe nothing. One of the main points Jesus aims to make is that everyone is to be considered a neighbor (no. 80). No exceptions.

Third, Jesus inverts the lawyer's question, replying, "Which of these three, do you think, was a neighbor to the man who fell into the hands of robbers?" In other words, the lawyer envisions the neighbor as the object of his duties while Jesus presents a vision of the neighbor as a proactively loving subject. This means the question we should ask is not, "Who is my neighbor?" but rather, "What kind of neighbor am I?" (And: "To whom am I a neighbor?")

Fourth, because we know this story so well, we might miss the fact that it plays on the particular location (the road to Jericho) that was notoriously unsafe. Jesus's audience has no sympathy for the man lying in the ditch. They're too busy judging him for traveling the road alone to be moved with compassion at his plight, making them more like the priest and Levite than the Samaritan. This also means that the Samaritan is exercising a special kind of courage in going into the ditch to care for the wounded man, since he could easily have been ambushed on this treacherous path. Since we see the term *Good Samaritan* on hospitals and soup kitchens and in news headlines, we might forget that Jews and Samaritans despised each other, so "Good Samaritan" would have been an absolute oxymoron for Jesus's audience. If we want to get a sense of their shock and dismay at hearing the Samaritan is the moral exemplar, we have to imagine someone detestable or dangerous, a person who makes our skin crawl or hair stand on end (no. 82).

Finally, the Samaritan models what it means to "love your neighbor as yourself" because unlike the priest and Levite who see the man left for dead and go to the other side of the road—creating greater distance between themselves and the one in need, becoming the "anti-neighbor"—the Samaritan goes out of his way and into the ditch. He draws near the robbers' victim, sharing a vulnerable position. To be like the Samaritan means straying from our normal paths and routines, reaching beyond our existing relationships, and being willing to companion those who may feel unseen or unheard, the insignificant and powerless. In a related vein, as we sit with this passage, we might more readily identify with the Samaritan or the person in the ditch, but due to local and global patterns of individualism, consumerism, unearned privilege, as well as other ways we benefit from injustice, it may be difficult to distinguish ourselves from the robbers. For this reason, the duties of solidarity require more than providing assistance to others in need; we must also commit to the kinds of practices and policies that prevent exclusion and exploitation, ensuring the full dignity, rights, and empowerment of each and every human being.

These features of the story invite us to pray with this passage and see ourselves in each of the characters. Pope Francis attests, "All of us have in ourselves something of the wounded man, something of the robber, something of the passers-by, and something of the Good Samaritan," which means that "each day we have to decide whether to be Good Samaritans or indifferent bystanders" (no. 69). After reviewing the characters in the story (nos. 72–76), Pope Francis encourages us to see each day as a new opportunity to model solidarity by emulating the Samaritan's "spirit of care and closeness" to those pushed to the peripheries of status, privilege, and power (no. 79). He reminds us of the parallel between Luke 10:25–37 and Matthew 25:31–46, where Jesus insists that what we do—or fail to do—for the neediest among us, we do—or fail to do—for him (no. 85). If we are to see Christ in others and be Christ for and with others, then our faith and practices of "catechesis and preaching" must "speak more directly and clearly about the social meaning of existence, the fraternal dimension of spirituality, our conviction of the inalienable dignity of each person, and our reasons for loving and accepting all our brothers and sisters" (no. 86).

---

56. The previous chapter should not be read as a cool and detached description of today's problems, for "the joys and hopes, the grief and anguish of the people of our time, especially of those who are poor or afflicted, are the joys and hopes, the grief and anguish of the followers of Christ as well. Nothing that is genuinely human fails to find an echo in their hearts."[53] In the attempt to search for a ray of light in the midst of what we

53. Second Vatican Ecumenical Council, Pastoral Constitution on the Church in the Modern World *Gaudium et Spes*, 1.

are experiencing, and before proposing a few lines of action, I now wish to devote a chapter to a parable told by Jesus Christ two thousand years ago. Although this Letter is addressed to all people of good will, regardless of their religious convictions, the parable is one that any of us can relate to and find challenging.

> "Just then a lawyer stood up to test Jesus. 'Teacher,' he said, 'what must I do to inherit eternal life?' He said to him, 'What is written in the law? What do you read there?' He answered, 'You shall love the Lord your God with all your heart, and with all your soul, and with all your strength, and with all your mind; and your neighbour as yourself.' And he said to him, 'You have given the right answer; do this, and you will live.' But wanting to justify himself, he asked Jesus, 'And who is my neighbour?' Jesus replied, 'A man was going down from Jerusalem to Jericho, and fell into the hands of robbers, who stripped him, beat him, and went away, leaving him half dead. Now by chance a priest was going down that road; and when he saw him, he passed by on the other side. So likewise a Levite, when he came to the place and saw him, passed by on the other side. But a Samaritan while traveling came near him; and when he saw him, he was moved with pity. He went to him and bandaged his wounds, having poured oil and wine on them. Then he put him on his own animal, brought him to an inn, and took care of him. The next day he took out two denarii, gave them to the innkeeper, and said, 'Take care of him; and when I come back, I will repay you whatever more you spend.' Which of these three, do you think, was a neighbour to the man who fell into the hands of the robbers?" He said, 'The one who showed him mercy.' Jesus said to him, 'Go and do likewise.'" (*Lk* 10:25–37)

The context

57. This parable has to do with an age-old problem. Shortly after its account of the creation of the world and of man, the Bible takes up the issue of human relationships. Cain kills his brother Abel and then hears God ask: "Where is your brother Abel?" (*Gen* 4:9). His answer is one that we ourselves all too often give: "Am I my brother's keeper?" (ibid.). By the very question he asks, God leaves no room for an appeal to determinism or fatalism as a justification for our own indifference. Instead, he encourages us to create a different culture, in which we resolve our conflicts and care for one another.

58. The Book of Job sees our origin in the one Creator as the basis of certain common rights: "Did not he who made me in the womb also make him? And did not the same one fashion us in the womb?" (*Job* 31:15). Many centuries later, Saint Irenaeus would use the image of a melody to make the same point: "One who seeks the truth should not concentrate on the differences between one note and another, thinking as if each was created separately and apart from the others; instead, he should realize that one and the same person composed the entire melody."[54]

59. In earlier Jewish traditions, the imperative to love and care for others appears to have been limited to relationships between members of the same nation. The ancient commandment to "love your neighbour as yourself" (*Lev* 19:18) was usually understood as referring to one's fellow citizens, yet the boundaries gradually expanded, especially in the Judaism that developed outside of the land of Israel. We encounter the command not to do to others what you would not want them to do to you (cf. *Tob* 4:15). In the first century before Christ, Rabbi Hillel stated: "This is the entire Torah. Everything else is commentary."[55] The desire to imitate God's own way of acting gradually replaced the tendency to think only of those nearest us: "The compassion of

54. Saint Irenaeus of Lyons, *Adversus Haereses*, II, 25, 2: PG 7/1, 798ff.
55. *Talmud Bavli* (Babylonian Talmud), *Shabbat*, 31a.

man is for his neighbour, but the compassion of the Lord is for all living beings" (*Sir* 18:13).

60. In the New Testament, Hillel's precept was expressed in positive terms: "In everything, do to others as you would have them do to you; for this is the law and the prophets" (*Mt* 7:12). This command is universal in scope, embracing everyone on the basis of our shared humanity, since the heavenly Father "makes his sun rise on the evil and on the good" (*Mt* 5:45). Hence the summons to "be merciful, just as your Father is merciful" (*Lk* 6:36).

61. In the oldest texts of the Bible, we find a reason why our hearts should expand to embrace the foreigner. It derives from the enduring memory of the Jewish people that they themselves had once lived as foreigners in Egypt:

> "You shall not wrong or oppress a stranger, for you were strangers in the land of Egypt" (*Ex* 22:21).
>
> "You shall not oppress a stranger; you know the heart of a stranger, for you were strangers in the land of Egypt" (*Ex* 23:9).
>
> "When a stranger resides with you in your land, you shall not do him wrong. The stranger who resides with you shall be to you as the citizen among you; you shall love the stranger as yourself, for you were strangers in the land of Egypt" (*Lev* 19:33–34).
>
> "When you gather the grapes of your vineyard, do not glean what is left; it shall be for the sojourner, the orphan, and the widow. Remember that you were a slave in the land of Egypt" (*Deut* 24:21–22).

The call to fraternal love echoes throughout the New Testament:

> "For the whole law is summed up in a single commandment, 'You shall love your neighbour as yourself'" (*Gal* 5:14).
>
> "Whoever loves a brother or sister lives in the light, and in such a person there is no cause for stum-

bling. But whoever hates another believer is in the darkness" (1 *Jn* 2:10–11).

"We know that we have passed from death to life because we love one another. Whoever does not love abides in death" (1 *Jn* 3:14).

"Those who do not love a brother or sister whom they have seen, cannot love God whom they have not seen" (1 *Jn* 4:20).

62. Yet this call to love could be misunderstood. Saint Paul, recognizing the temptation of the earliest Christian communities to form closed and isolated groups, urged his disciples to abound in love "for one another and for all" (1 *Thess* 3:12). In the Johannine community, fellow Christians were to be welcomed, "even though they are strangers to you" (3 *Jn* 5). In this context, we can better understand the significance of the parable of the Good Samaritan: love does not care if a brother or sister in need comes from one place or another. For "love shatters the chains that keep us isolated and separate; in their place, it builds bridges. Love enables us to create one great family, where all of us can feel at home... Love exudes compassion and dignity."[56]

> "Love does not care if a brother or sister in need comes from one place or another...love shatters the chains that keep us isolated and separate; in their place, it builds bridges. Love enables us to create one great family, where all of us can feel at home... Love exudes compassion and dignity" (no. 62).

Abandoned on the wayside

63. Jesus tells the story of a man assaulted by thieves and lying injured on the wayside. Several persons passed him by, but

56. *Address to Those Assisted by the Charitable Works of the Church*, Tallinn, Estonia (25 September 2018): *L'Osservatore Romano*, 27 September 2018, p. 8.

failed to stop. These were people holding important social positions, yet lacking in real concern for the common good. They would not waste a couple of minutes caring for the injured man, or even in calling for help. Only one person stopped, approached the man and cared for him personally, even spending his own money to provide for his needs. He also gave him something that in our frenetic world we cling to tightly: he gave him his time. Certainly, he had his own plans for that day, his own needs, commitments and desires. Yet he was able to put all that aside when confronted with someone in need. Without even knowing the injured man, he saw him as deserving of his time and attention.

64. Which of these persons do you identify with? This question, blunt as it is, is direct and incisive. Which of these characters do you resemble? We need to acknowledge that we are constantly tempted to ignore others, especially the weak. Let us admit that, for all the progress we have made, we are still "illiterate" when it comes to accompanying, caring for and supporting the most frail and vulnerable members of our developed societies. We have become accustomed to looking the other way, passing by, ignoring situations until they affect us directly.

> "Which of these persons do you identify with? This question, blunt as it is, is direct and incisive. Which of these characters do you resemble? We need to acknowledge that we are constantly tempted to ignore others, especially the weak. Let us admit that, for all the progress we have made, we are still 'illiterate' when it comes to accompanying, caring for and supporting the most frail and vulnerable members of our developed societies. We have become accustomed to looking the other way, passing by, ignoring situations until they affect us directly" (no. 64).

65. Someone is assaulted on our streets, and many hurry off as if they did not notice. People hit someone with their car

and then flee the scene. Their only desire is to avoid problems; it does not matter that, through their fault, another person could die. All these are signs of an approach to life that is spreading in various and subtle ways. What is more, caught up as we are with our own needs, the sight of a person who is suffering disturbs us. It makes us uneasy, since we have no time to waste on other people's problems. These are symptoms of an unhealthy society. A society that seeks prosperity but turns its back on suffering.

66. May we not sink to such depths! Let us look to the example of the Good Samaritan. Jesus' parable summons us to rediscover our vocation as citizens of our respective nations and of the entire world, builders of a new social bond. This summons is ever new, yet it is grounded in a fundamental law of our being: we are called to direct society to the pursuit of the common good and, with this purpose in mind, to persevere in consolidating its political and social order, its fabric of relations, its human goals. By his actions, the Good Samaritan showed that "the existence of each and every individual is deeply tied to that of others: life is not simply time that passes; life is a time for interactions."[57]

67. The parable eloquently presents the basic decision we need to make in order to rebuild our wounded world. In the face of so much pain and suffering, our only course is to imitate the Good Samaritan. Any other decision would make us either one of the robbers or one of those who walked by without showing compassion for the sufferings of the man on the roadside. The parable shows us how a community can be rebuilt by men and women who identify with the vulnerability of others, who reject the creation of a society of exclusion, and act instead as neighbours, lifting up and rehabilitating the fallen for the sake of the common good. At the same time, it warns us about the attitude of those who think only of themselves and fail to shoulder the inevitable responsibilities of life as it is.

57. *Video Message to the TED Conference in Vancouver* (26 April 2017): *L'Osservatore Romano*, 27 April 2017, p. 7.

> "The parable eloquently presents the basic decision we need to make in order to rebuild our wounded world. In the face of so much pain and suffering, our only course is to imitate the Good Samaritan. Any other decision would make us either one of the robbers or one of those who walked by without showing compassion for the sufferings of the man on the roadside. The parable shows us how a community can be rebuilt by men and women who identify with the vulnerability of others, who reject the creation of a society of exclusion, and act instead as neighbors, lifting up and rehabilitating the fallen for the sake of the common good. At the same time, it warns us about the attitude of those who think only of themselves and fail to shoulder the inevitable responsibilities of life as it is" (no. 67).

68. The parable clearly does not indulge in abstract moralizing, nor is its message merely social and ethical. It speaks to us of an essential and often forgotten aspect of our common humanity: we were created for a fulfilment that can only be found in love. We cannot be indifferent to suffering; we cannot allow anyone to go through life as an outcast. Instead, we should feel indignant, challenged to emerge from our comfortable isolation and to be changed by our contact with human suffering. That is the meaning of dignity.

A story constantly retold

69. The parable is clear and straightforward, yet it also evokes the interior struggle that each of us experiences as we gradually come to know ourselves through our relationships with our brothers and sisters. Sooner or later, we will all encounter a person who is suffering. Today there are more and more of them. The decision to include or exclude those lying wounded along the roadside can serve as a criterion for judging every economic,

political, social and religious project. Each day we have to decide whether to be Good Samaritans or indifferent bystanders. And if we extend our gaze to the history of our own lives and that of the entire world, all of us are, or have been, like each of the characters in the parable. All of us have in ourselves something of the wounded man, something of the robber, something of the passers-by, and something of the Good Samaritan.

70. It is remarkable how the various characters in the story change, once confronted by the painful sight of the poor man on the roadside. The distinctions between Judean and Samaritan, priest and merchant, fade into insignificance. Now there are only two kinds of people: those who care for someone who is hurting and those who pass by; those who bend down to help and those who look the other way and hurry off. Here, all our distinctions, labels and masks fall away: it is the moment of truth. Will we bend down to touch and heal the wounds of others? Will we bend down and help another to get up? This is today's challenge, and we should not be afraid to face it. In moments of crisis, decisions become urgent. It could be said that, here and now, anyone who is neither a robber nor a passer-by is either injured himself or bearing an injured person on his shoulders.

71. The story of the Good Samaritan is constantly being repeated. We can see this clearly as social and political inertia are turning many parts of our world into a desolate byway, even as domestic and international disputes and the robbing of opportunities are leaving great numbers of the marginalized stranded on the roadside. In his parable, Jesus does not offer alternatives; he does not ask what might have happened had the injured man or the one who helped him yielded to anger or a thirst for revenge. Jesus trusts in the best of the human spirit; with this parable, he encourages us to persevere in love, to restore dignity to the suffering and to build a society worthy of the name.

The characters of the story

72. The parable begins with the robbers. Jesus chose to start when the robbery has already taken place, lest we dwell on the

crime itself or the thieves who committed it. Yet we know them well. We have seen, descending on our world, the dark shadows of neglect and violence in the service of petty interests of power, gain and division. The real question is this: will we abandon the injured man and run to take refuge from the violence, or will we pursue the thieves? Will the wounded man end up being the justification for our irreconcilable divisions, our cruel indifference, our intestine conflicts?

73. The parable then asks us to take a closer look at the passers-by. The nervous indifference that makes them pass to the other side of the road—whether innocently or not, whether the result of disdain or mere distraction—makes the priest and the Levite a sad reflection of the growing gulf between ourselves and the world around us. There are many ways to pass by at a safe distance: we can retreat inwards, ignore others, or be indifferent to their plight. Or simply look elsewhere, as in some countries, or certain sectors of them, where contempt is shown for the poor and their culture, and one looks the other way, as if a development plan imported from without could edge them out. This is how some justify their indifference: the poor, whose pleas for help might touch their hearts, simply do not exist. The poor are beyond the scope of their interest.

74. One detail about the passers-by does stand out: they were religious, devoted to the worship of God: a priest and a Levite. This detail should not be overlooked. It shows that belief in God and the worship of God are not enough to ensure that we are actually living in a way pleasing to God. A believer may be untrue to everything that his faith demands of him, and yet think he is close to God and better than others. The guarantee of an authentic openness to God, on the other hand, is a way of practising the faith that helps open our hearts to our brothers and sisters. Saint John Chrysostom expressed this pointedly when he challenged his Christian hearers: "Do you wish to honour the body of the Saviour? Do not despise it when it is naked. Do not honour it in church with silk vestments while outside it is

naked and numb with cold."[58] Paradoxically, those who claim to be unbelievers can sometimes put God's will into practice better than believers.

> "Belief in God and the worship of God are not enough to ensure that we are actually living in a way pleasing to God. A believer may be untrue to everything that his faith demands of him, and yet think he is close to God and better than others. The guarantee of an authentic openness to God, on the other hand, is a way of practicing the faith that helps open our hearts to our brothers and sisters" (no. 74).

75. "Robbers" usually find secret allies in those who "pass by and look the other way." There is a certain interplay between those who manipulate and cheat society, and those who, while claiming to be detached and impartial critics, live off that system and its benefits. There is a sad hypocrisy when the impunity of crime, the use of institutions for personal or corporate gain, and other evils apparently impossible to eradicate, are accompanied by a relentless criticism of everything, a constant sowing of suspicion that results in distrust and confusion. The complaint that "everything is broken" is answered by the claim that "it can't be fixed," or "what can I do?" This feeds into disillusionment and despair, and hardly encourages a spirit of solidarity and generosity. Plunging people into despair closes a perfectly perverse circle: such is the agenda of the invisible dictatorship of hidden interests that have gained mastery over both resources and the possibility of thinking and expressing opinions.

76. Let us turn at last to the injured man. There are times when we feel like him, badly hurt and left on [the] side of the road. We can also feel helpless because our institutions are neglected and lack resources, or simply serve the interests of a few, without

58. *Homiliae in Matthaeum*, 50: 3–4: PG 58, 508.

and within. Indeed, "globalized society often has an elegant way of shifting its gaze. Under the guise of being politically correct or ideologically fashionable, we look at those who suffer without touching them. We televise live pictures of them, even speaking about them with euphemisms and with apparent tolerance."[59]

Starting anew

77. Each day offers us a new opportunity, a new possibility. We should not expect everything from those who govern us, for that would be childish. We have the space we need for co-responsibility in creating and putting into place new processes and changes. Let us take an active part in renewing and supporting our troubled societies. Today we have a great opportunity to express our innate sense of fraternity, to be Good Samaritans who bear the pain of other people's troubles rather than fomenting greater hatred and resentment. Like the chance traveller in the parable, we need only have a pure and simple desire to be a people, a community, constant and tireless in the effort to include, integrate and lift up the fallen. We may often find ourselves succumbing to the mentality of the violent, the blindly ambitious, those who spread mistrust and lies. Others may continue to view politics or the economy as an arena for their own power plays. For our part, let us foster what is good and place ourselves at its service.

78. We can start from below and, case by case, act at the most concrete and local levels, and then expand to the farthest reaches of our countries and our world, with the same care and concern that the Samaritan showed for each of the wounded man's injuries. Let us seek out others and embrace the world as it is, without fear of pain or a sense of inadequacy, because there we will discover all the goodness that God has planted in human hearts. Difficulties that seem overwhelming are opportunities for growth, not excuses for a glum resignation that can lead only

---

59. *Message to the Meeting of Popular Movements*, Modesto, California, United States of America (10 February 2017): AAS 109 (2017), 291.

to acquiescence. Yet let us not do this alone, as individuals. The Samaritan discovered an innkeeper who would care for the man; we too are called to unite as a family that is stronger than the sum of small individual members. For "the whole is greater than the part, but it is also greater than the sum of its parts."[60] Let us renounce the pettiness and resentment of useless in-fighting and constant confrontation. Let us stop feeling sorry for ourselves and acknowledge our crimes, our apathy, our lies. Reparation and reconciliation will give us new life and set us all free from fear.

79. The Samaritan who stopped along the way departed without expecting any recognition or gratitude. His effort to assist another person gave him great satisfaction in life and before his God, and thus became a duty. All of us have a responsibility for the wounded, those of our own people and all the peoples of the earth. Let us care for the needs of every man and woman, young and old, with the same fraternal spirit of care and closeness that marked the Good Samaritan.

Neighbours without borders

80. Jesus told the parable of the Good Samaritan in answer to the question: Who is my neighbour? The word "neighbour," in the society of Jesus' time, usually meant those nearest us. It was felt that help should be given primarily to those of one's own group and race. For some Jews of that time, Samaritans were looked down upon, considered impure. They were not among those to be helped. Jesus, himself a Jew, completely transforms this approach. He asks us not to decide who is close enough to be our neighbour, but rather that we ourselves become neighbours to all.

81. Jesus asks us to be present to those in need of help, regardless of whether or not they belong to our social group. In this case, the Samaritan *became a neighbour* to the wounded Judean. By approaching and making himself present, he crossed all cultural and historical barriers. Jesus concludes the parable by saying: "Go

60. Apostolic Exhortation *Evangelii Gaudium* (24 November 2013), 235: AAS 105 (2013), 1115.

and do likewise" (*Lk* 10:37). In other words, he challenges us to put aside all differences and, in the face of suffering, to draw near to others with no questions asked. I should no longer say that I have neighbours to help, but that I must myself be a neighbour to others.

> "Jesus concludes the parable by saying: 'Go and do likewise' (*Lk* 10:37). In other words, he challenges us to put aside all differences and, in the face of suffering, to draw near to others with no questions asked. I should no longer say that I have neighbours to help, but that I must myself be a neighbour to others" (no. 81).

82. The parable, though, is troubling, for Jesus says that the wounded man was a Judean, while the one who stopped and helped him was a Samaritan. This detail is quite significant for our reflection on a love that includes everyone. The Samaritans lived in a region where pagan rites were practised. For the Jews, this made them impure, detestable, dangerous. In fact, one ancient Jewish text referring to nations that were hated, speaks of Samaria as "not even a people" (*Sir* 50:25); it also refers to "the foolish people that live in Shechem" (50:26).

83. This explains why a Samaritan woman, when asked by Jesus for a drink, answered curtly: "How is it that you, a Jew, ask a drink of me, a woman of Samaria?" (*Jn* 4:9). The most offensive charge that those who sought to discredit Jesus could bring was that he was "possessed" and "a Samaritan" (*Jn* 8:48). So this encounter of mercy between a Samaritan and a Jew is highly provocative; it leaves no room for ideological manipulation and challenges us to expand our frontiers. It gives a universal dimension to our call to love, one that transcends all prejudices, all historical and cultural barriers, all petty interests.

The plea of the stranger

84. Finally, I would note that in another passage of the Gospel

Jesus says: "I was a stranger and you welcomed me" (*Mt* 25:35). Jesus could speak those words because he had an open heart, sensitive to the difficulties of others. Saint Paul urges us to "rejoice with those who rejoice, weep with those who weep" (*Rom* 12:15). When our hearts do this, they are capable of identifying with others without worrying about where they were born or come from. In the process, we come to experience others as our "own flesh" (*Is* 58:7).

85. For Christians, the words of Jesus have an even deeper meaning. They compel us to recognize Christ himself in each of our abandoned or excluded brothers and sisters (cf. *Mt* 25:40.45). Faith has untold power to inspire and sustain our respect for others, for believers come to know that God loves every man and woman with infinite love and "thereby confers infinite dignity" upon all humanity.[61] We likewise believe that Christ shed his blood for each of us and that no one is beyond the scope of his universal love. If we go to the ultimate source of that love which is the very life of the triune God, we encounter in the community of the three divine Persons the origin and perfect model of all life in society. Theology continues to be enriched by its reflection on this great truth.

86. I sometimes wonder why, in light of this, it took so long for the Church unequivocally to condemn slavery and various forms of violence. Today, with our developed spirituality and theology, we have no excuses. Still, there are those who appear to feel encouraged or at least permitted by their faith to support varieties of narrow and violent nationalism, xenophobia and contempt, and even the mistreatment of those who are different. Faith, and the humanism it inspires, must maintain a critical sense in the face of these tendencies, and prompt an immediate response whenever they rear their head. For this reason, it is important that catechesis and preaching speak more directly and clearly about the social meaning of existence, the fraternal dimension of spirituality,

61. Saint John Paul II, *Message to the Handicapped, Angelus* in Osnabrück, Germany (16 November 1980): *Insegnamenti* III, 2 (1980), 1232.

our conviction of the inalienable dignity of each person, and our reasons for loving and accepting all our brothers and sisters.

QUESTIONS FOR REFLECTION AND DISCUSSION

1. What does Pope Francis add to your thoughts about this passage from Luke's Gospel and how does it compare to some of the most transformative encounters in your life? What do you observe in the encounters that left a lasting impression on you? Who is a person or group that is difficult for you to recognize as a neighbor—and why? What does it say about our belief in God when we acknowledge those we might discriminate against or condemn? What might change if you try to see this person or group as God sees them: as infinitely loved and conferred with infinite dignity (no. 85)?
2. Pope Francis summarizes the meaning of Luke 10:25–37 in this way: "We were created for a fulfillment that can only be found in love. We cannot be indifferent to suffering; we cannot allow anyone to go through life as an outcast. Instead, we should feel indignant, challenged to emerge from our comfortable isolation and to be changed by our contact with human suffering" (no. 68). How do you respond to these claims? What do you affirm—and why? What would you contest or question—and why? How would you translate this vision of discipleship into your life in a concrete manner?
3. Pope Francis reminds us, "We should not expect everything from those who govern us, for that would be childish. We have the space we need for co-responsibility in creating and putting into place new processes and changes.

Let us take an active part in renewing and supporting our troubled societies" (no. 77). Nothing changes if nothing changes; how is Pope Francis inviting you to consider the ways that God can make change possible through your thoughts, feelings, words, and actions? What are steps you can take to try to be more attentive and responsive to these opportunities for personal and social change?

4. Sometimes we let ourselves off the hook too easily, making excuses for why we don't draw near to others in need (no. 64). We might be convinced that we're too busy and already stretched thin, or we might be plagued with self-doubt: Who am I to offer any help? What good can I do? How can we find a balance between expecting too much and not enough from ourselves? What are ways we can "rediscover our vocation as citizens of our respective nations and of the entire world, builders of a new social bond" (no. 66)?
5. Notice that Jesus's parting lines are "Go and do likewise" (Luke 10:37). This does not mean "Go and do exactly the same." Instead, it is a challenge to creatively imagine how we can replicate the Samaritan's courage, compassion, and boundary-breaking solidarity according to our means. As you reflect and pray with this passage, how can you listen and look for ways that God is calling and empowering you to "do likewise" in your context, doing what you can—no more and no less?

FOR FURTHER READING

Clark, Meghan J. *The Vision of Catholic Social Thought: The Virtue of Solidarity and the Praxis of Human Rights*. Minneapolis: Fortress Press, 2014.

Heyer, Kristin E. *Kinship across Borders: A Christian Ethic of*

Immigration. Washington, DC: Georgetown University Press, 2012.

King, Jr. Martin Luther. *Strength to Love*. Minneapolis: Fortress Press, 1963/2010.

Mescher, Marcus. *The Ethics of Encounter: Christian Neighbor Love as a Practice of Solidarity*. Maryknoll, NY: Orbis Books, 2020.

O'Connell, Maureen H. *Compassion: Loving Our Neighbor in an Age of Globalization*. Maryknoll, NY: Orbis Books, 2009.

Chapter Three

ENVISAGING AND ENGENDERING AN OPEN WORLD

SYNOPSIS

The third chapter of *Fratelli Tutti* continues the theological reflection that comprises the third step of the pastoral spiral. It reads like a summary of the foundations of Catholic social teaching, starting with the dignity of the human person and moving on to the exercise of rights and responsibilities for the common good. The opening paragraphs proceed following an insight Pope Francis imparts near the end of the second chapter: a theology of solidarity finds its basis in the Trinity, a communion of love. The pope explains, "If we go to the ultimate source of that love which is the very life of the triune God, we encounter in the community of the three divine Persons the origin and perfect model of all life in society" (no. 85). In contrast to the self-interest, disregard, mistrust, and discord that plague the cultural anthropology—as outlined in the first chapter—this section of the encyclical presents a Christian vision of humanity rooted in the claim that every human person is a reflection and representative of, as well as internally related to the triune God. In simplest terms: "we were made for love" (no. 88) and the "spiritual stature of a person's life is measured by love" (no. 92). Citing Aquinas's insight that the effect of love is union, we should think of love not only as an emotion but a commitment to take effective action for the well-being of those whom we love (no. 94). Solidarity accentuates the social dimension of love, a "social friendship that excludes no one," a kinship "open to all" in mutual belonging that strives for "universal communion" (nos. 94–95).

Moving from a posture oriented toward inclusion and unity, Pope Francis pivots toward paying special attention to those on the peripheries. These can be persons who are "hidden exiles" in our cities and towns, people trapped in poverty or experiencing homelessness, living with disabilities or a chronic health condition, and especially the elderly (no. 98). They are also the people and communities who bear the brunt of racism, which "lurks in waiting" (no. 97). Illustrating the preferential option for the vulnerable, the pope insists that we respond not with token gestures of concern or quick fixes, but dedicate ourselves to the "demanding and even tiring process" of attending to people on the margins as "unique and unrepeatable" persons, creating the conditions for full and equal participation so that each person can be an agent of their own future (no. 98).

The next section examines tensions between freedom and equality, especially in the face of toxic individualism that views the human person more as a monad than as ordered to the reciprocity of relationships and a mutual investment in the common good (no. 111). This is not simply a distinction between cultural and theological anthropology, but a matter of moral responsibility to deliver what is good for each and all (nos. 112–13). Then the pope turns his focus to solidarity as a moral virtue, an orientation toward community, and a "way of making history" through "universal consciousness and mutual concern" in economics and politics (nos. 114–17). He suggests that the first step toward solidarity lies in service to people in need, but we fall well short of the goal if our service does not inform our advocacy to combat the systems that perpetuate inequality and poverty, unemployment and homelessness, and inadequate access to education and healthcare.

The final paragraphs of this chapter provide a summary of some of the foundations of Catholic social teaching: the right to private property relative to the universal destination of all goods (nos. 118–20); the right to migrate, the duty to provide hospitality, and the necessity of orienting business and industry to collective development (nos. 121–23); and inherent rights that are not confined to or contingent upon nationality, requiring a "new network of international relations" (nos. 124–27). Without a spiritual lens to see ourselves as equal in dignity and belonging to God's family—even across borders—the pope acknowledges that "what I am saying here will sound wildly unrealistic" (no. 127). This chapter outlines the logic of solidarity that begins with inherent human dignity as the basis for both inalienable human rights and moral duties deliver on the rights of others. It sets up the next chapter, Pope Francis's appeal to our hearts to tap into the moral will to realize this vision in our time and place.

---

87. Human beings are so made that they cannot live, develop and find fulfilment except "in the sincere gift of self to others."[62] Nor can they fully know themselves apart from an encounter with other persons: "I communicate effectively with myself only

62. Second Vatican Ecumenical Council, Pastoral Constitution on the Church in the Modern World *Gaudium et Spes*, 24.

insofar as I communicate with others."[63] No one can experience the true beauty of life without relating to others, without having real faces to love. This is part of the mystery of authentic human existence. "Life exists where there is bonding, communion, fraternity; and life is stronger than death when it is built on true relationships and bonds of fidelity. On the contrary, there is no life when we claim to be self-sufficient and live as islands: in these attitudes, death prevails."[64]

MOVING BEYOND OURSELVES

88. In the depths of every heart, love creates bonds and expands existence, for it draws people out of themselves and towards others.[65] Since we were made for love, in each one of us "a law of *ekstasis*" seems to operate: "the lover 'goes outside' the self to find a fuller existence in another."[66] For this reason, "man always has to take up the challenge of moving beyond himself."[67]

89. Nor can I reduce my life to relationships with a small group, even my own family; I cannot know myself apart from a broader network of relationships, including those that have preceded me and shaped my entire life. My relationship with those whom I respect has to take account of the fact that they do not live only for me, nor do I live only for them. Our relationships, if healthy and authentic, open us to others who expand and enrich us. Nowadays, our noblest social instincts can easily be thwarted by self-centred chats that give the impression of being deep relationships. On the contrary, authentic and mature love and true

63. Gabriel Marcel, *Du refus à l'invocation*, ed. NRF, Paris, 1940, 50.

64. *Angelus* (10 November 2019): *L'Osservatore Romano*, 11–12 November 2019, 8.

65. Cf. Saint Thomas Aquinas: *Scriptum super Sententiis*, lib. 3, dist. 27, q. 1, a. 1, ad 4: "Dicitur amor extasim facere et fervere, quia quod fervet extra se bullit et exhalat."

66. Karol Wojtyła, *Love and Responsibility*, London, 1982, 126.

67. Karl Rahner, *Kleines Kirchenjahr. Ein Gang durch den Festkreis*, Herderbücherei 901, Freiburg, 1981, 30.

friendship can only take root in hearts open to growth through relationships with others. As couples or friends, we find that our hearts expand as we step out of ourselves and embrace others. Closed groups and self-absorbed couples that define themselves in opposition to others tend to be expressions of selfishness and mere self-preservation.

90. Significantly, many small communities living in desert areas developed a remarkable system of welcoming pilgrims as an exercise of the sacred duty of hospitality. The medieval monastic communities did likewise, as we see from the Rule of Saint Benedict. While acknowledging that it might detract from the discipline and silence of monasteries, Benedict nonetheless insisted that "the poor and pilgrims be treated with the utmost care and attention."[68] Hospitality was one specific way of rising to the challenge and the gift present in an encounter with those outside one's own circle. The monks realized that the values they sought to cultivate had to be accompanied by a readiness to move beyond themselves in openness to others.

The unique value of love

91. People can develop certain habits that might appear as moral values: fortitude, sobriety, hard work and similar virtues. Yet if the acts of the various moral virtues are to be rightly directed, one needs to take into account the extent to which they foster openness and union with others. That is made possible by the charity that God infuses. Without charity, we may perhaps possess only apparent virtues, incapable of sustaining life in common. Thus, Saint Thomas Aquinas could say—quoting Saint Augustine—that the temperance of a greedy person is in no way virtuous.[69] Saint Bonaventure, for his part, explained that

68. *Regula*, 53, 15: "*Pauperum et peregrinorum maxime susceptioni cura sollicite exhibeatur.*"

69. Cf. *Summa Theologiae*, II–II, q. 23, a. 7; Saint Augustine, *Contra Julianum*, 4, 18: PL 44, 748: "How many pleasures do misers forego, either to increase their treasures or for fear of seeing them diminish!"

the other virtues, without charity, strictly speaking do not fulfil the commandments "the way God wants them to be fulfilled."[70]

92. The spiritual stature of a person's life is measured by love, which in the end remains "the criterion for the definitive decision about a human life's worth or lack thereof."[71] Yet some believers think that it consists in the imposition of their own ideologies upon everyone else, or in a violent defence of the truth, or in impressive demonstrations of strength. All of us, as believers, need to recognize that love takes first place: love must never be put at risk, and the greatest danger lies in failing to love (cf. *1 Cor* 13:1–13).

> "The spiritual stature of a person's life is measured by love, which in the end remains 'the criterion for the definitive decision about a human life's worth or lack thereof.' Yet some believers think that it consists in the imposition of their own ideologies upon everyone else, or in a violent defense of the truth, or in impressive demonstrations of strength. All of us, as believers, need to recognize that love takes first place: love must never be put at risk, and the greatest danger lies in failing to love (cf. *1 Cor* 13:1–13)" (no. 92).

93. Saint Thomas Aquinas sought to describe the love made possible by God's grace as a movement outwards towards another, whereby we consider "the beloved as somehow united to ourselves."[72] Our affection for others makes us freely desire to seek their good. All this originates in a sense of esteem, an appreciation of the value of the other. This is ultimately the idea behind the word "charity": those who are loved are "dear" to me; "they

70. "*Secundum acceptionem divinam*" (*Scriptum super Sententiis*, lib. 3, dist. 27, a. 1, q. 1, concl. 4).

71. Benedict XVI, Encyclical Letter *Deus Caritas Est* (25 December 2005), 15: AAS 98 (2006), 230.

72. *Summa Theologiae* II–II, q. 27, a. 2, resp.

are considered of great value."[73] And "the love whereby someone becomes pleasing (*grata*) to another is the reason why the latter bestows something on him freely (*gratis*)."[74]

94. Love, then, is more than just a series of benevolent actions. Those actions have their source in a union increasingly directed towards others, considering them of value, worthy, pleasing and beautiful apart from their physical or moral appearances. Our love for others, for who they *are*, moves us to seek the best for their lives. Only by cultivating this way of relating to one another will we make possible a social friendship that excludes no one and a fraternity that is open to all.

A LOVE EVER MORE OPEN

95. Love also impels us towards universal communion. No one can mature or find fulfilment by withdrawing from others. By its very nature, love calls for growth in openness and the ability to accept others as part of a continuing adventure that makes every periphery converge in a greater sense of mutual belonging. As Jesus told us: "You are all brothers" (*Mt* 23:8).

96. This need to transcend our own limitations also applies to different regions and countries. Indeed, "the ever-increasing number of interconnections and communications in today's world makes us powerfully aware of the unity and common destiny of the nations. In the dynamics of history, and in the diversity of ethnic groups, societies and cultures, we see the seeds of a vocation to form a community composed of brothers and sisters who accept and care for one another."[75]

Open societies that integrate everyone

97. Some peripheries are close to us, in city centres or within our families. Hence there is an aspect of universal openness in

73. Cf. ibid., I–II, q. 26, a. 3, resp.

74. Ibid., q. 110, a. 1, resp.

75. *Message for the 2014 World Day of Peace* (8 December 2013), 1: AAS 106 (2014), 22.

love that is existential rather than geographical. It has to do with our daily efforts to expand our circle of friends, to reach those who, even though they are close to me, I do not naturally consider a part of my circle of interests. Every brother or sister in need, when abandoned or ignored by the society in which I live, becomes an existential foreigner, even though born in the same country. They may be citizens with full rights, yet they are treated like foreigners in their own country. Racism is a virus that quickly mutates and, instead of disappearing, goes into hiding, and lurks in waiting.

98. I would like to mention some of those "hidden exiles" who are treated as foreign bodies in society.[76] Many persons with disabilities "feel that they exist without belonging and without participating." Much still prevents them from being fully enfranchised. Our concern should be not only to care for them but to ensure their "active participation in the civil and ecclesial community. That is a demanding and even tiring process, yet one that will gradually contribute to the formation of consciences capable of acknowledging each individual as a unique and unrepeatable person." I think, too, of "the elderly who, also due to their disability, are sometimes considered a burden." Yet each of them is able to offer "a unique contribution to the common good through their remarkable life stories." Let me repeat: we need to have "the courage to give a voice to those who are discriminated against due to their disability, because sadly, in some countries even today, people find it hard to acknowledge them as persons of equal dignity."[77]

Inadequate understandings of universal love

99. A love capable of transcending borders is the basis of what in every city and country can be called "social friendship."

76. Cf. *Angelus* (29 December 2013): *L'Osservatore Romano*, 30–31 December 2013, p. 7; *Address to the Diplomatic Corps Accredited to the Holy See* (12 January 2015): AAS 107 (2015), 165.

77. *Message for the World Day of Persons with Disabilities* (3 December 2019): *L'Osservatore Romano*, 4 December 2019, 7.

Genuine social friendship within a society makes true universal openness possible. This is a far cry from the false universalism of those who constantly travel abroad because they cannot tolerate or love their own people. Those who look down on their own people tend to create within society categories of first and second class, people of greater or lesser dignity, people enjoying greater or fewer rights. In this way, they deny that there is room for everybody.

100. I am certainly not proposing an authoritarian and abstract universalism, devised or planned by a small group and presented as an ideal for the sake of levelling, dominating and plundering. One model of globalization in fact "consciously aims at a one-dimensional uniformity and seeks to eliminate all differences and traditions in a superficial quest for unity... If a certain kind of globalization claims to make everyone uniform, to level everyone out, that globalization destroys the rich gifts and uniqueness of each person and each people."[78] This false universalism ends up depriving the world of its various colours, its beauty and, ultimately, its humanity. For "the future is not monochrome; if we are courageous, we can contemplate it in all the variety and diversity of what each individual person has to offer. How much our human family needs to learn to live together in harmony and peace, without all of us having to be the same!"[79]

BEYOND A WORLD OF "ASSOCIATES"

101. Let us now return to the parable of the Good Samaritan, for it still has much to say to us. An injured man lay on the roadside. The people walking by him did not heed their interior summons to act as neighbours; they were concerned with their

---

78. *Address to the Meeting for Religious Liberty with the Hispanic Community and Immigrant Groups*, Philadelphia, Pennsylvania, United States of America (26 September 2015): AAS 107 (2015), 1050–1051.

79. *Address to Young People*, Tokyo, Japan (25 November 2019): *L'Osservatore Romano*, 25–26 November 2019, 10.

duties, their social status, their professional position within society. They considered themselves important for the society of the time, and were anxious to play their proper part. The man on the roadside, bruised and abandoned, was a distraction, an interruption from all that; in any event, he was hardly important. He was a "nobody," undistinguished, irrelevant to their plans for the future. The Good Samaritan transcended these narrow classifications. He himself did not fit into any of those categories; he was simply a foreigner without a place in society. Free of every label and position, he was able to interrupt his journey, change his plans, and unexpectedly come to the aid of an injured person who needed his help.

102. What would be the reaction to that same story nowadays, in a world that constantly witnesses the emergence and growth of social groups clinging to an identity that separates them from others? How would it affect those who organize themselves in a way that prevents any foreign presence that might threaten their identity and their closed and self-referential structures? There, even the possibility of acting as a neighbour is excluded; one is a neighbour only to those who serve their purpose. The word "neighbour" loses all meaning; there can only be "associates," partners in the pursuit of particular interests.[80]

Liberty, equality and fraternity

103. Fraternity is born not only of a climate of respect for individual liberties, or even of a certain administratively guaranteed equality. Fraternity necessarily calls for something greater, which in turn enhances freedom and equality. What happens when fraternity is not consciously cultivated, when there is a lack of political will to promote it through education in fraternity, through dialogue and through the recognition of the values of reciprocity and mutual enrichment? Liberty becomes nothing

80. In these considerations, I have been inspired by the thought of Paul Ricoeur, "Le socius et le prochain," in *Histoire et Verité*, ed. Le Seuil, Paris, 1967, 113–127.

more than a condition for living as we will, completely free to choose to whom or what we will belong, or simply to possess or exploit. This shallow understanding has little to do with the richness of a liberty directed above all to love.

104. Nor is equality achieved by an abstract proclamation that "all men and women are equal." Instead, it is the result of the conscious and careful cultivation of fraternity. Those capable only of being "associates" create closed worlds. Within that framework, what place is there for those who are not part of one's group of associates, yet long for a better life for themselves and their families?

105. Individualism does not make us more free, more equal, more fraternal. The mere sum of individual interests is not capable of generating a better world for the whole human family. Nor can it save us from the many ills that are now increasingly globalized. Radical individualism is a virus that is extremely difficult to eliminate, for it is clever. It makes us believe that everything consists in giving free rein to our own ambitions, as if by pursuing ever greater ambitions and creating safety nets we would somehow be serving the common good.

"Individualism does not make us more free, more equal, more fraternal. The mere sum of individual interests is not capable of generating a better world for the whole human family. Nor can it save us from the many ills that are now increasingly globalized. Radical individualism is a virus that is extremely difficult to eliminate, for it is clever. It makes us believe that everything consists in giving free rein to our own ambitions, as if by pursuing ever greater ambitions and creating safety nets we would somehow be serving the common good" (no. 105).

A UNIVERSAL LOVE THAT PROMOTES PERSONS

106. Social friendship and universal fraternity necessarily call for an acknowledgement of *the worth of every human person*, always and everywhere. If each individual is of such great worth, it must be stated clearly and firmly that "the mere fact that some people are born in places with fewer resources or less development does not justify the fact that they are living with less dignity."[81] This is a basic principle of social life that tends to be ignored in a variety of ways by those who sense that it does not fit into their worldview or serve their purposes.

107. Every human being has the right to live with dignity and to develop integrally; this fundamental right cannot be denied by any country. People have this right even if they are unproductive, or were born with or developed limitations. This does not detract from their great dignity as human persons, a dignity based not on circumstances but on the intrinsic worth of their being. Unless this basic principle is upheld, there will be no future either for fraternity or for the survival of humanity.

108. Some societies accept this principle in part. They agree that opportunities should be available to everyone, but then go on to say that everything depends on the individual. From this skewed perspective, it would be pointless "to favour an investment in efforts to help the slow, the weak or the less talented to find opportunities in life."[82] Investments in assistance to the vulnerable could prove unprofitable; they might make things less efficient. No. What we need in fact are states and civil institutions that are present and active, that look beyond the free and efficient working of certain economic, political or ideological systems, and are primarily concerned with individuals and the common good.

109. Some people are born into economically stable families, receive a fine education, grow up well nourished, or naturally

81. Apostolic Exhortation *Evangelii Gaudium* (24 November 2013), 190: AAS 105 (2013), 1100.

82. Ibid., 209: AAS 105 (2013), 1107.

possess great talent. They will certainly not need a proactive state; they need only claim their freedom. Yet the same rule clearly does not apply to a disabled person, to someone born in dire poverty, to those lacking a good education and with little access to adequate health care. If a society is governed primarily by the criteria of market freedom and efficiency, there is no place for such persons, and fraternity will remain just another vague ideal.

110. Indeed, "to claim economic freedom while real conditions bar many people from actual access to it, and while possibilities for employment continue to shrink, is to practice "doublespeak."[83] Words like freedom, democracy or fraternity prove meaningless, for the fact is that "only when our economic and social system no longer produces even a single victim, a single person cast aside, will we be able to celebrate the feast of universal fraternity."[84] A truly human and fraternal society will be capable of ensuring in an efficient and stable way that each of its members is accompanied at every stage of life. Not only by providing for their basic needs, but by enabling them to give the best of themselves, even though their performance may be less than optimum, their pace slow or their efficiency limited.

111. The human person, with his or her inalienable rights, is by nature open to relationship. Implanted deep within us is the call to transcend ourselves through an encounter with others. For this reason, "care must be taken not to fall into certain errors which can arise from a misunderstanding of the concept of human rights and from its misuse. Today there is a tendency to claim ever broader individual—I am tempted to say individualistic—rights. Underlying this is a conception of the human person as detached from all social and anthropological contexts, as if the person were a "monad" (*monás*), increasingly unconcerned with others... Unless the rights of each individual are harmoniously ordered to the greater good,

83. Encyclical Letter *Laudato Si'* (24 May 2015), 129: AAS 107 (2015), 899.

84. *Message for the "Economy of Francesco" Event* (1 May 2019): *L'Osservatore Romano*, 12 May 2019, 8.

those rights will end up being considered limitless and consequently will become a source of conflicts and violence."[85]

PROMOTING THE MORAL GOOD

112. Nor can we fail to mention that seeking and pursuing the good of others and of the entire human family also implies helping individuals and societies to mature in the moral values that foster integral human development. The New Testament describes one fruit of the Holy Spirit (cf. *Gal* 5:22) as *agathosyne*; the Greek word expresses attachment to the good, pursuit of the good. Even more, it suggests a striving for excellence and what is best for others, their growth in maturity and health, the cultivation of values and not simply material wellbeing. A similar expression exists in Latin: *benevolentia*. This is an attitude that "wills the good" of others; it bespeaks a yearning for goodness, an inclination towards all that is fine and excellent, a desire to fill the lives of others with what is beautiful, sublime and edifying.

113. Here, regrettably, I feel bound to reiterate that "we have had enough of immorality and the mockery of ethics, goodness, faith and honesty. It is time to acknowledge that light-hearted superficiality has done us no good. Once the foundations of social life are corroded, what ensues are battles over conflicting interests."[86] Let us return to promoting the good, for ourselves and for the whole human family, and thus advance together towards an authentic and integral growth. Every society needs to ensure that values are passed on; otherwise, what is handed down are selfishness, violence, corruption in its various forms, indifference and, ultimately, a life closed to transcendence and entrenched in individual interests.

---

85. *Address to the European Parliament*, Strasbourg (25 November 2014): AAS 106 (2014), 997.

86. Encyclical Letter *Laudato Si'* (24 May 2015), 229: AAS 107 (2015), 937.

The value of solidarity

114. I would like especially to mention solidarity, which, "as a moral virtue and social attitude born of personal conversion, calls for commitment on the part of those responsible for education and formation. I think first of families, called to a primary and vital mission of education. Families are the first place where the values of love and fraternity, togetherness and sharing, concern and care for others are lived out and handed on. They are also the privileged milieu for transmitting the faith, beginning with those first simple gestures of devotion which mothers teach their children. Teachers, who have the challenging task of training children and youth in schools or other settings, should be conscious that their responsibility extends also to the moral, spiritual and social aspects of life. The values of freedom, mutual respect and solidarity can be handed on from a tender age... Communicators also have a responsibility for education and formation, especially nowadays, when the means of information and communication are so widespread."[87]

115. At a time when everything seems to disintegrate and lose consistency, it is good for us to appeal to the "solidity"[88] born of the consciousness that we are responsible for the fragility of others as we strive to build a common future. Solidarity finds concrete expression in service, which can take a variety of forms in an effort to care for others. And service in great part means "caring for vulnerability, for the vulnerable members of our families, our society, our people." In offering such service, individuals learn to "set aside their own wishes and desires, their pursuit of power, before the concrete gaze of those who are most vulnerable... Service always looks to their faces, touches their flesh, senses their closeness and even, in some cases, 'suffers' that closeness and

87. *Message for the 2016 World Day of Peace* (8 December 2015), 6: AAS 108 (2016), 57–58.

88. Solidity is etymologically related to "solidarity." Solidarity, in the ethical-political meaning that it has taken on in the last two centuries, results in a secure and firm social compact.

tries to help them. Service is never ideological, for we do not serve ideas, we serve people."[89]

116. The needy generally "practise the special solidarity that exists among those who are poor and suffering, and which our civilization seems to have forgotten or would prefer in fact to forget. Solidarity is a word that is not always well received; in certain situations, it has become a dirty word, a word that dare not be said. Solidarity means much more than engaging in sporadic acts of generosity. It means thinking and acting in terms of community. It means that the lives of all are prior to the appropriation of goods by a few. It also means combatting the structural causes of poverty, inequality, the lack of work, land and housing, the denial of social and labour rights. It means confronting the destructive effects of the empire of money... Solidarity, understood in its most profound meaning, is a way of making history, and this is what popular movements are doing."[90]

117. When we speak of the need to care for our common home, our planet, we appeal to that spark of universal consciousness and mutual concern that may still be present in people's hearts. Those who enjoy a surplus of water yet choose to conserve it for the sake of the greater human family have attained a moral stature that allows them to look beyond themselves and the group to which they belong. How marvellously human! The same attitude is demanded if we are to recognize the rights of all people, even those born beyond our own borders.

RE-ENVISAGING THE SOCIAL ROLE OF PROPERTY

118. The world exists for everyone, because all of us were born with the same dignity. Differences of colour, religion, talent,

89. *Homily*, Havana, Cuba (20 September 2015): *L'Osservatore Romano*, 21–22 September 2015, 8.

90. *Address to Participants in the Meeting of Popular Movements* (28 October 2014): AAS 106 (2014), 851–852.

place of birth or residence, and so many others, cannot be used to justify the privileges of some over the rights of all. As a community, we have an obligation to ensure that every person lives with dignity and has sufficient opportunities for his or her integral development.

> "The world exists for everyone, because all of us were born with the same dignity. Differences of color, religion, talent, place of birth or residence, and so many others, cannot be used to justify the privileges of some over the rights of all. As a community, we have an obligation to ensure that every person lives with dignity and has sufficient opportunities for his or her integral development" (no. 118).

119. In the first Christian centuries, a number of thinkers developed a universal vision in their reflections on the common destination of created goods.[91] This led them to realize that if one person lacks what is necessary to live with dignity, it is because another person is detaining it. Saint John Chrysostom summarizes it in this way: "Not to share our wealth with the poor is to rob them and take away their livelihood. The riches we possess are not our own, but theirs as well."[92] In the words of Saint Gregory the Great, "When we provide the needy with their basic needs, we are giving them what belongs to them, not to us."[93]

120. Once more, I would like to echo a statement of Saint John Paul II whose forcefulness has perhaps been insufficiently recognized: "God gave the earth to the whole human race for the sustenance of all its members, without excluding or favouring

91. Cf. Saint Basil, *Homilia XXI, Quod rebus mundanis adhaerendum non sit*, 3.5: PG 31, 545–549; *Regulae brevius tractatae*, 92: PG 31, 1145–1148; Saint Peter Chrysologus, *Sermo* 123: PL 52, 536–540; Saint Ambrose, *De Nabuthe*, 27.52: PL 14, 738ff.; Saint Augustine, *In Iohannis Evangelium*, 6, 25: PL 35, 1436ff.

92. *De Lazaro Concio*, II, 6: PG 48, 992D.

93. *Regula Pastoralis*, III, 21: PL 77, 87.

anyone."[94] For my part, I would observe that "the Christian tradition has never recognized the right to private property as absolute or inviolable, and has stressed the social purpose of all forms of private property."[95] The principle of the common use of created goods is the "first principle of the whole ethical and social order";[96] it is a natural and inherent right that takes priority over others.[97] All other rights having to do with the goods necessary for the integral fulfilment of persons, including that of private property or any other type of property, should—in the words of Saint Paul VI—"in no way hinder [this right], but should actively facilitate its implementation."[98] The right to private property can only be considered a secondary natural right, derived from the principle of the universal destination of created goods. This has concrete consequences that ought to be reflected in the workings of society. Yet it often happens that secondary rights displace primary and overriding rights, in practice making them irrelevant.

Rights without borders

121. No one, then, can remain excluded because of his or her place of birth, much less because of privileges enjoyed by others who were born in lands of greater opportunity. The limits and borders of individual states cannot stand in the way of this. As it is unacceptable that some have fewer rights by virtue of being women, it is likewise unacceptable that the mere place of one's birth or residence should result in his or her possessing fewer opportunities for a developed and dignified life.

122. Development must not aim at the amassing of wealth by a few, but must ensure "human rights—personal and social,

94. Saint John Paul II, Encyclical Letter *Centesimus Annus* (1 May 1991), 31: AAS 83 (1991), 831.

95. Encyclical Letter *Laudato Si'* (24 May 2015), 93: AAS 107 (2015), 884.

96. Saint John Paul II, Encyclical Letter *Laborem Exercens* (14 September 1981), 19: AAS 73 (1981), 626.

97. Cf. Pontifical Council for Justice and Peace, *Compendium of the Social Doctrine of the Church*, 172.

98. Encyclical Letter *Populorum Progressio* (26 March 1967): AAS 59 (1967), 268.

economic and political, including the rights of nations and of peoples."[99] The right of some to free enterprise or market freedom cannot supersede the rights of peoples and the dignity of the poor, or, for that matter, respect for the natural environment, for "if we make something our own, it is only to administer it for the good of all."[100]

123. Business activity is essentially "a noble vocation, directed to producing wealth and improving our world."[101] God encourages us to develop the talents he gave us, and he has made our universe one of immense potential. In God's plan, each individual is called to promote his or her own development,[102] and this includes finding the best economic and technological means of multiplying goods and increasing wealth. Business abilities, which are a gift from God, should always be clearly directed to the development of others and to eliminating poverty, especially through the creation of diversified work opportunities. The right to private property is always accompanied by the primary and prior principle of the subordination of all private property to the universal destination of the earth's goods, and thus the right of all to their use.[103]

The rights of peoples

124. Nowadays, a firm belief in the common destination of the earth's goods requires that this principle also be applied to nations, their territories and their resources. Seen from the standpoint not only of the legitimacy of private property and the rights of its citizens, but also of the first principle of the common

99. Saint John Paul II, Encyclical Letter *Sollicitudo Rei Socialis* (30 December 1987), 33: AAS 80 (1988), 557.

100. Encyclical Letter *Laudato Si'* (24 May 2015), 95: AAS 107 (2015), 885.

101. Ibid., 129: AAS 107 (2015), 899.

102. Cf. Saint Paul VI, Encyclical Letter *Populorum Progressio* (26 March 1967): AAS 59 (1967), 265; Benedict XVI, Encyclical Letter *Caritas in Veritate* (29 June 2009), 16: AAS 101 (2009), 652.

103. Cf. Encyclical Letter *Laudato Si'* (24 May 2015), 93: AAS 107 (2015), 884–885; Apostolic Exhortation *Evangelii Gaudium* (24 November 2013), 189–190: AAS 105 (2013), 1099–1100.

destination of goods, we can then say that each country also belongs to the foreigner, inasmuch as a territory's goods must not be denied to a needy person coming from elsewhere. As the Bishops of the United States have taught, there are fundamental rights that "precede any society because they flow from the dignity granted to each person as created by God."[104]

125. This presupposes a different way of understanding relations and exchanges between countries. If every human being possesses an inalienable dignity, if all people are my brothers and sisters, and if the world truly belongs to everyone, then it matters little whether my neighbour was born in my country or elsewhere. My own country also shares responsibility for his or her development, although it can fulfil that responsibility in a variety of ways. It can offer a generous welcome to those in urgent need, or work to improve living conditions in their native lands by refusing to exploit those countries or to drain them of natural resources, backing corrupt systems that hinder the dignified development of their peoples. What applies to nations is true also for different regions within each country, since there too great inequalities often exist. At times, the inability to recognize equal human dignity leads the more developed regions in some countries to think that they can jettison the "dead weight" of poorer regions and so increase their level of consumption.

> "If every human being possesses an inalienable dignity, if all people are my brothers and sisters, and if the world truly belongs to everyone, then it matters little whether my neighbor was born in my country or elsewhere. My own country also shares responsibility for his or her development, although it can fulfil that responsibility in a variety of ways. It can offer a generous welcome to those in urgent need, or work to improve living conditions in their native lands by

104. United States Conference of Catholic Bishops, Pastoral Letter Against Racism *Open Wide Our Hearts: The Enduring Call to Love* (November 2018).

refusing to exploit those countries or to drain them of natural resources, backing corrupt systems that hinder the dignified development of their peoples" (no. 125).

126. We are really speaking about a new network of international relations, since there is no way to resolve the serious problems of our world if we continue to think only in terms of mutual assistance between individuals or small groups. Nor should we forget that "inequity affects not only individuals but entire countries; it compels us to consider an ethics of international relations."[105] Indeed, justice requires recognizing and respecting not only the rights of individuals, but also social rights and the rights of peoples.[106] This means finding a way to ensure "the fundamental right of peoples to subsistence and progress,"[107] a right which is at times severely restricted by the pressure created by foreign debt. In many instances, debt repayment not only fails to promote development but gravely limits and conditions it. While respecting the principle that all legitimately acquired debt must be repaid, the way in which many poor countries fulfil this obligation should not end up compromising their very existence and growth.

127. Certainly, all this calls for an alternative way of thinking. Without an attempt to enter into that way of thinking, what I am saying here will sound wildly unrealistic. On the other hand, if we accept the great principle that there are rights born of our inalienable human dignity, we can rise to the challenge of envisaging a new humanity. We can aspire to a world that provides land, housing and work for all. This is the true path of peace, not the senseless and myopic strategy of sowing fear and mistrust in the face of outside threats. For a real and lasting peace will only be possible "on the basis of a global ethic of solidarity and cooperation

105. Encyclical Letter *Laudato Si'* (24 May 2015), 51: AAS 107 (2015), 867.

106. Cf. Benedict XVI, Encyclical Letter *Caritas in Veritate* (29 June 2009), 6: AAS 101 (2009), 644.

107. Saint John Paul II, Encyclical Letter *Centesimus Annus* (1 May 1991), 35: AAS 83 (1991), 838.

in the service of a future shaped by interdependence and shared responsibility in the whole human family."[108]

> "All this calls for an alternative way of thinking. Without an attempt to enter into that way of thinking, what I am saying here will sound wildly unrealistic. On the other hand, if we accept the great principle that there are rights born of our inalienable human dignity, we can rise to the challenge of envisaging a new humanity. We can aspire to a world that provides land, housing and work for all. This is the true path of peace" (no. 127).

QUESTIONS FOR REFLECTION AND DISCUSSION

1. How do you respond to the claim that "we were made for love" (no. 88)? Where do you look in your life for evidence of this claim—and why? What experience or relationship makes this difficult to accept? How are you being challenged to witness being made for love in your life—and help others discover this truth for themselves, too?
2. The pope states that love "impels us towards universal communion. No one can mature or find fulfillment by withdrawing from others. By its very nature, love calls for growth in openness and the ability to accept others as part of a continuing adventure that makes every periphery converge in a greater sense of mutual belonging" (no. 95). However, due to our inherent limitations, the need for self-care, and our duties to those who rely on us the most (like family, friends, and coworkers), we

108. *Address on Nuclear Weapons*, Nagasaki, Japan (24 November 2019): *L'Osservatore Romano*, 25–26 November 2019, 6.

cannot be open to everyone we meet. Moreover, while some encounters are illuminating and life-giving, others leave us scarred and suspicious. How do you know how to balance how much you avail yourself to others without the risk of overextending yourself or making yourself susceptible to be used or abused by others?

3. How do you understand the relationship between dignity, rights, and duties? Some rights are more about protection (requiring freedom from influence, interference, or coercion) while others necessitate access to a particular good or service (that must be provided to individuals and communities, like education, a minimum wage, or the access to vote). What does this section of *Fratelli Tutti* add to your thinking about how authentic freedom requires both kinds of rights—and what you owe others and are owed from others?
4. In paragraphs 101–2, Pope Francis returns to the example of the Samaritan to emphasize his ability to "transcend narrow classifications" or labels. How do we honor differences between individuals and groups without letting these differences eclipse what we share in common? What would it take for the concept of "neighbor" to help us see beyond categories (like "liberal" or "conservative") and embrace the "great worth" (no. 106) of every person, regardless of belief or behavior?
5. Pope Francis contends, "Solidarity is a word that is not always well received; in certain situations, it has become a dirty word, a word that dare not be said. Solidarity means much more than engaging in sporadic acts of generosity. It means thinking and acting in terms of community" (no. 116). How could we make progress toward this paradigm shift from self-interest to communal wellbeing? How do you assess the pope's concern this sounds

"wildly unrealistic" (no. 127)—and what would help this find traction in your social context?

FOR FURTHER READING

Ahlgren, Gillian T. W. *The Tenderness of God: Reclaiming Our Humanity*. Minneapolis: Fortress Press, 2017.

Camosy, Charles C. *Resisting Throwaway Culture: How a Consistent Life Ethic Can Unite a Fractured People*. Hyde Park, NY: New City Press, 2019.

Copeland, Shawn M. *Enfleshing Freedom: Body, Race, and Being*. Minneapolis: Fortress Press, 2010.

Kammer, Fred. *Doing Faithjustice: An Introduction to Catholic Social Thought*. New York: Paulist Press, 2004.

Massaro, Thomas. *Living Justice: Catholic Social Teaching in Action*. Lanham, MD: Rowman & Littlefield, 2016.

Chapter Four

A HEART OPEN TO THE WHOLE WORLD

SYNOPSIS

This chapter bridges the third and fourth steps of the pastoral spiral, capping theological reflection and inspiring a pastoral response through a conversion of our hearts. Pope Francis explains, "If the conviction that all human beings are brothers and sisters is not to remain an abstract idea but to find concrete embodiment, then numerous related issues emerge, forcing us to see things in a new light and to develop new responses" (no. 128). If solidarity is to avoid being disregarded as "wildly unrealistic" (no. 127), then we have to experience the *metanoia* that turns our hearts away from idols of comfort and convenience, status and admiration, money and power. We also have to persist in the ongoing conversion that moves us from imagining that solidarity is possible to actualizing solidarity in the world.

Conversion is only possible through the integration of our minds, hearts, and hands. For this reason, Pope Francis moves from solidarity as a concept to solidarity in action, as exemplified in his 2017 "Share the Journey" campaign to encourage hospitality to refugees and migrants. This initiative featured four verbs: "welcome, protect, promote, and integrate" (no. 129), depicting the "concrete embodiment" that incarnates solidarity in the world. Solidarity moves from theory to practice in bringing people together to welcome strangers displaced from their homes, protecting their legal rights, promoting their participation in society, and integrating them into the "culture of encounter" through intercultural exchange. Every encounter is an opportunity to engage or ignore the other, just as we decide whether or not to make ourselves available to be engaged by others. But if we close ourselves off to the gifts we have to offer and receive from others, the status quo remains unchanged. To open up thresholds for encounter, Pope Francis urges us to embrace the "reciprocal gifts" that await us in adopting a "fruitful exchange" between individuals and nations. He reminds us that indifference and isolation only impoverish our experience of life, if not imperil it; he reiterates his assertion that "we need to develop the awareness that nowadays we are either all saved together or no one is saved" (no. 137).

In the face of so much busyness, so many concerns about scarce opportunities and resources, it can seem like generosity is reserved only for the affluent. Pope Francis confronts this temptation by reminding us of God's gratuitous providence and superabundant love (Matt 5:45; 10:8). Since God loves us without condition or limitation, God also enables us to live magnanimously. We have no reason to feel like a disappointment or fear that we are not measuring up in God's eyes, and we should extend this gracious posture of acceptance and affirmation to others. This is what it means to "be merciful, just as your Father is merciful" (Luke 6:36). Or, as the pope translates this for our social reality, "Only a social and political culture that readily and 'gratuitously' welcomes others will have a future" (no. 141).

This chapter concludes by underscoring a necessary tension between the local and global (nos. 142–50). These are not alternative options or competing poles, but two sides of the same coin in human experience: the universality of a single human family that is called to communion strong enough to hold together—and be enriched by—a great diversity of particular places and perspectives. His appeal to a conversion in solidarity is ultimately an appeal to affix our gaze on a "universal horizon" that gives us a common heading as we step into the future. This requires a bold openness that does not risk one's identity (no. 148). On the contrary, openness to growth, to learning from and with others "brings the joyful realization that no one people, culture or individual can achieve everything on its own: to attain fulfilment in life we need others" (no. 150). This insight is worth our careful reflection, prayer, and discussion; how many of us feel anxious or insecure due to our limitations? Instead of seeing our limits as flaws or weaknesses, this vision of solidarity sees them as reminders that we are not self-sufficient. Our limits point to the need for encounter and exchange, for reciprocity and mutuality so we can be in right-relationship with others. Despite St. Paul's boast that he became "all things to all" people (1 Cor 9:22), God does not expect us to transcend our finite knowledge and abilities. This should be a liberating realization, a joyful discovery: our limits are gifts that keep us from expecting too much of ourselves—and others. And yet, this focus on conversion keeps us from settling for anything less than what God makes possible in and through us.

---

128. If the conviction that all human beings are brothers and sisters is not to remain an abstract idea but to find concrete

embodiment, then numerous related issues emerge, forcing us to see things in a new light and to develop new responses.

BORDERS AND THEIR LIMITS

129. Complex challenges arise when our neighbour happens to be an immigrant.[109] Ideally, unnecessary migration ought to be avoided; this entails creating in countries of origin the conditions needed for a dignified life and integral development. Yet until substantial progress is made in achieving this goal, we are obliged to respect the right of all individuals to find a place that meets their basic needs and those of their families, and where they can find personal fulfilment. Our response to the arrival of migrating persons can be summarized by four words: welcome, protect, promote and integrate. For "it is not a case of implementing welfare programmes from the top down, but rather of undertaking a journey together, through these four actions, in order to build cities and countries that, while preserving their respective cultural and religious identity, are open to differences and know how to promote them in the spirit of human fraternity."[110]

> "Our response to the arrival of migrating persons can be summarized by four words: welcome, protect, promote and integrate. For 'it is not a case of implementing welfare programs from the top down, but rather of undertaking a journey together, through these four actions, in order to build cities and countries that, while preserving their respective cultural and religious identity, are open to differences and know how to promote them in the spirit of human fraternity'" (no. 129).

109. Cf. Catholic Bishops of Mexico and the United States, *A Pastoral Letter Concerning Migration: "Strangers No Longer Together on the Journey of Hope"* (January 2003).

110. *General Audience* (3 April 2019): *L'Osservatore Romano*, 4 April 2019, p. 8.

130. This implies taking certain indispensable steps, especially in response to those who are fleeing grave humanitarian crises. As examples, we may cite: increasing and simplifying the granting of visas; adopting programmes of individual and community sponsorship; opening humanitarian corridors for the most vulnerable refugees; providing suitable and dignified housing; guaranteeing personal security and access to basic services; ensuring adequate consular assistance and the right to retain personal identity documents; equitable access to the justice system; the possibility of opening bank accounts and the guarantee of the minimum needed to survive; freedom of movement and the possibility of employment; protecting minors and ensuring their regular access to education; providing for programmes of temporary guardianship or shelter; guaranteeing religious freedom; promoting integration into society; supporting the reuniting of families; and preparing local communities for the process of integration.[111]

131. For those who are not recent arrivals and already participate in the fabric of society, it is important to apply the concept of "citizenship," which "is based on the equality of rights and duties, under which all enjoy justice. It is therefore crucial to establish in our societies the concept of *full citizenship* and to reject the discriminatory use of the term *minorities*, which engenders feelings of isolation and inferiority. Its misuse paves the way for hostility and discord; it undoes any successes and takes away the religious and civil rights of some citizens who are thus discriminated against."[112]

132. Even when they take such essential steps, states are not able, on their own, to implement adequate solutions, "since the consequences of the decisions made by each inevitably have repercussions on the entire international community." As a result,

111. Cf. *Message for the 2018 World Day of Migrants and Refugees* (14 January 2018): AAS 109 (2017), 918–923.

112. *Document on Human Fraternity for World Peace and Living Together*, Abu Dhabi (4 February 2019): *L'Osservatore Romano*, 4–5 February 2019, p. 7.

"our response can only be the fruit of a common effort"[113] to develop a form of global governance with regard to movements of migration. Thus, there is "a need for mid-term and long-term planning which is not limited to emergency responses. Such planning should include effective assistance for integrating migrants in their receiving countries, while also promoting the development of their countries of origin through policies inspired by solidarity, yet not linking assistance to ideological strategies and practices alien or contrary to the cultures of the peoples being assisted."[114]

RECIPROCAL GIFTS

133. The arrival of those who are different, coming from other ways of life and cultures, can be a gift, for "the stories of migrants are always stories of an encounter between individuals and between cultures. For the communities and societies to which they come, migrants bring an opportunity for enrichment and the integral human development of all."[115] For this reason, "I especially urge young people not to play into the hands of those who would set them against other young people, newly arrived in their countries, and who would encourage them to view the latter as a threat, and not possessed of the same inalienable dignity as every other human being."[116]

134. Indeed, when we open our hearts to those who are different, this enables them, while continuing to be themselves, to develop in new ways. The different cultures that have flourished over the centuries need to be preserved, lest our world be impoverished. At the same time, those cultures should be encouraged to be open to new experiences through their encounter with other realities, for the risk of succumbing to cultural sclerosis is

113. *Address to the Diplomatic Corps Accredited to the Holy See*, 11 January 2016: AAS 108 (2016), 124.

114. Ibid., 122.

115. Post-Synodal Apostolic Exhortation *Christus Vivit* (25 March 2019), 93.

116. Ibid., 94.

always present. That is why "we need to communicate with each other, to discover the gifts of each person, to promote that which unites us, and to regard our differences as an opportunity to grow in mutual respect. Patience and trust are called for in such dialogue, permitting individuals, families and communities to hand on the values of their own culture and welcome the good that comes from others' experiences."[117]

135. Here I would mention some examples that I have used in the past. Latino culture is "a ferment of values and possibilities that can greatly enrich the United States," for "intense immigration always ends up influencing and transforming the culture of a place... In Argentina, intense immigration from Italy has left a mark on the culture of the society, and the presence of some 200,000 Jews has a great effect on the cultural 'style' of Buenos Aires. Immigrants, if they are helped to integrate, are a blessing, a source of enrichment and new gift that encourages a society to grow."[118]

136. On an even broader scale, Grand Imam Ahmad Al-Tayyeb and I have observed that "good relations between East and West are indisputably necessary for both. They must not be neglected, so that each can be enriched by the other's culture through fruitful exchange and dialogue. The West can discover in the East remedies for those spiritual and religious maladies that are caused by a prevailing materialism. And the East can find in the West many elements that can help free it from weakness, division, conflict and scientific, technical and cultural decline. It is important to pay attention to religious, cultural and historical differences that are a vital component in shaping the character, culture and civilization of the East. It is likewise important to reinforce the bond of fundamental human rights in order to help ensure a dignified life for all the men and women of East and West, avoiding the politics of double standards."[119]

117. *Address to Authorities*, Sarajevo, Bosnia and Herzegovina (6 June 2015): *L'Osservatore Romano*, 7 June 2015, p. 7.

118. *Latinoamérica. Conversaciones con Hernán Reyes Alcaide*, ed. Planeta, Buenos Aires, 2017, 105.

119. *Document on Human Fraternity for World Peace and Living Together*, Abu Dhabi (4 February 2019): *L'Osservatore Romano*, 4–5 February 2019, p. 7.

A fruitful exchange

137. Mutual assistance between countries proves enriching for each. A country that moves forward while remaining solidly grounded in its original cultural substratum is a treasure for the whole of humanity. We need to develop the awareness that nowadays we are either all saved together or no one is saved. Poverty, decadence and suffering in one part of the earth are a silent breeding ground for problems that will end up affecting the entire planet. If we are troubled by the extinction of certain species, we should be all the more troubled that in some parts of our world individuals or peoples are prevented from developing their potential and beauty by poverty or other structural limitations. In the end, this will impoverish us all.

> "We need to develop the awareness that nowadays we are either all saved together or no one is saved. Poverty, decadence and suffering in one part of the earth are a silent breeding ground for problems that will end up affecting the entire planet. If we are troubled by the extinction of certain species, we should be all the more troubled that in some parts of our world individuals or peoples are prevented from developing their potential and beauty by poverty or other structural limitations. In the end, this will impoverish us all" (no. 137).

138. Although this has always been true, never has it been more evident than in our own day, when the world is interconnected by globalization. We need to attain a global juridical, political and economic order "which can increase and give direction to international cooperation for the development of all peoples in solidarity."[120] Ultimately, this will benefit the entire world, since "development aid for poor countries" implies "creating wealth

120. Benedict XVI, Encyclical Letter *Caritas in Veritate* (29 June 2009), 67: AAS 101 (2009), 700.

for all."[121] From the standpoint of integral development, this presupposes "giving poorer nations an effective voice in shared decision-making"[122] and the capacity to "facilitate access to the international market on the part of countries suffering from poverty and underdevelopment."[123]

A gratuitousness open to others

139. Even so, I do not wish to limit this presentation to a kind of utilitarian approach. There is always the factor of "gratuitousness": the ability to do some things simply because they are good in themselves, without concern for personal gain or recompense. Gratuitousness makes it possible for us to welcome the stranger, even though this brings us no immediate tangible benefit. Some countries, though, presume to accept only scientists or investors.

140. Life without fraternal gratuitousness becomes a form of frenetic commerce, in which we are constantly weighing up what we give and what we get back in return. God, on the other hand, gives freely, to the point of helping even those who are unfaithful; he "makes his sun rise on the evil and on the good" (*Mt* 5:45). There is a reason why Jesus told us: "When you give alms, do not let your right hand know what your left hand is doing, so that your alms may be in secret" (*Mt* 6:3–4). We received life freely; we paid nothing for it. Consequently, all of us are able to give without expecting anything in return, to do good to others without demanding that they treat us well in return. As Jesus told his disciples: "Without cost you have received, without cost you are to give" (*Mt* 10:8).

141. The true worth of the different countries of our world is measured by their ability to think not simply as a country but also as part of the larger human family. This is seen especially in times of crisis. Narrow forms of nationalism are an extreme expression of an inability to grasp the meaning of this gratuitousness. They err in

121. Ibid., 60: AAS 101 (2009), 695.

122. Ibid., 67: AAS 101 (2009), 700.

123. Pontifical Council for Justice and Peace, *Compendium of the Social Doctrine of the Church*, 447.

thinking that they can develop on their own, heedless of the ruin of others, that by closing their doors to others they will be better protected. Immigrants are seen as usurpers who have nothing to offer. This leads to the simplistic belief that the poor are dangerous and useless, while the powerful are generous benefactors. Only a social and political culture that readily and "gratuitously" welcomes others will have a future.

LOCAL AND UNIVERSAL

142. It should be kept in mind that "an innate tension exists between globalization and localization. We need to pay attention to the global so as to avoid narrowness and banality. Yet we also need to look to the local, which keeps our feet on the ground. Together, the two prevent us from falling into one of two extremes. In the first, people get caught up in an abstract, globalized universe... In the other, they turn into a museum of local folklore, a world apart, doomed to doing the same things over and over, incapable of being challenged by novelty or appreciating the beauty which God bestows beyond their borders."[124] We need to have a global outlook to save ourselves from petty provincialism. When our house stops being a home and starts to become an enclosure, a cell, then the global comes to our rescue, like a "final cause" that draws us towards our fulfilment. At the same time, though, the local has to be eagerly embraced, for it possesses something that the global does not: it is capable of being a leaven, of bringing enrichment, of sparking mechanisms of subsidiarity. Universal fraternity and social friendship are thus two inseparable and equally vital poles in every society. To separate them would be to disfigure each and to create a dangerous polarization.

---

124. Apostolic Exhortation *Evangelii Gaudium* (24 November 2013), 234: AAS 105 (2013), 1115.

Local flavour

143. The solution is not an openness that spurns its own richness. Just as there can be no dialogue with "others" without a sense of our own identity, so there can be no openness between peoples except on the basis of love for one's own land, one's own people, one's own cultural roots. I cannot truly encounter another unless I stand on firm foundations, for it is on the basis of these that I can accept the gift the other brings and in turn offer an authentic gift of my own. I can welcome others who are different, and value the unique contribution they have to make, only if I am firmly rooted in my own people and culture. Everyone loves and cares for his or her native land and village, just as they love and care for their home and are personally responsible for its upkeep. The common good likewise requires that we protect and love our native land. Otherwise, the consequences of a disaster in one country will end up affecting the entire planet. All this brings out the positive meaning of the right to property: I care for and cultivate something that I possess, in such a way that it can contribute to the good of all.

144. It also gives rise to healthy and enriching exchanges. The experience of being raised in a particular place and sharing in a particular culture gives us insight into aspects of reality that others cannot so easily perceive. Universal does not necessarily mean bland, uniform and standardized, based on a single prevailing cultural model, for this will ultimately lead to the loss of a rich palette of shades and colours, and result in utter monotony. Such was the temptation referred to in the ancient account of the Tower of Babel. The attempt to build a tower that would reach to heaven was not an expression of unity between various peoples speaking to one another from their diversity. Instead, it was a misguided attempt, born of pride and ambition, to create a unity other than that willed by God in his providential plan for the nations (cf. *Gen* 11:1–9).

145. There can be a false openness to the universal, born of the shallowness of those lacking insight into the genius of their native land or harbouring unresolved resentment towards their

own people. Whatever the case, "we constantly have to broaden our horizons and see the greater good which will benefit us all. But this has to be done without evasion or uprooting. We need to sink our roots deeper into the fertile soil and history of our native place, which is a gift of God. We can work on a small scale, in our own neighbourhood, but with a larger perspective... The global need not stifle, nor the particular prove barren";[125] our model must be that of a polyhedron, in which the value of each individual is respected, where "the whole is greater than the part, but it is also greater than the sum of its parts."[126]

A universal horizon

146. There is a kind of "local" narcissism unrelated to a healthy love of one's own people and culture. It is born of a certain insecurity and fear of the other that leads to rejection and the desire to erect walls for self-defence. Yet it is impossible to be "local" in a healthy way without being sincerely open to the universal, without feeling challenged by what is happening in other places, without openness to enrichment by other cultures, and without solidarity and concern for the tragedies affecting other peoples. A "local narcissism" instead frets over a limited number of ideas, customs and forms of security; incapable of admiring the vast potential and beauty offered by the larger world, it lacks an authentic and generous spirit of solidarity. Life on the local level thus becomes less and less welcoming, people less open to complementarity. Its possibilities for development narrow; it grows weary and infirm. A healthy culture, on the other hand, is open and welcoming by its very nature; indeed, "a culture without universal values is not truly a culture."[127]

147. Let us realize that as our minds and hearts narrow, the less capable we become of understanding the world around us. Without encountering and relating to differences, it is hard to

125. Ibid., 235: AAS 105 (2013), 1115.

126. Ibid.

127. Saint John Paul II, *Address to Representatives of Argentinian Culture*, Buenos Aires, Argentina (12 April 1987), 4: *L'Osservatore Romano*, 14 April 1987, p. 7.

achieve a clear and complete understanding even of ourselves and of our native land. Other cultures are not "enemies" from which we need to protect ourselves, but differing reflections of the inexhaustible richness of human life. Seeing ourselves from the perspective of another, of one who is different, we can better recognize our own unique features and those of our culture: its richness, its possibilities and its limitations. Our local experience needs to develop "in contrast to" and "in harmony with" the experiences of others living in diverse cultural contexts.[128]

> "Let us realize that as our minds and hearts narrow, the less capable we become of understanding the world around us. Without encountering and relating to differences, it is hard to achieve a clear and complete understanding even of ourselves and of our native land. Other cultures are not "enemies" from which we need to protect ourselves, but differing reflections of the inexhaustible richness of human life. Seeing ourselves from the perspective of another, of one who is different, we can better recognize our own unique features and those of our culture: its richness, its possibilities and its limitations" (no. 147).

148. In fact, a healthy openness never threatens one's own identity. A living culture, enriched by elements from other places, does not import a mere carbon copy of those new elements, but integrates them in its own unique way. The result is a new synthesis that is ultimately beneficial to all, since the original culture itself ends up being nourished. That is why I have urged indigenous peoples to cherish their roots and their ancestral cultures. At the same time, though, I have wanted to stress that I have no intention of proposing "a completely enclosed, a-historic, static 'indigenism' that would reject any kind of blending (*mestizaje*)."

128. Cf. ID., *Address to the Roman Curia* (21 December 1984), 4: AAS 76 (1984), 506.

For "our own cultural identity is strengthened and enriched as a result of dialogue with those unlike ourselves. Nor is our authentic identity preserved by an impoverished isolation."[129] The world grows and is filled with new beauty, thanks to the successive syntheses produced between cultures that are open and free of any form of cultural imposition.

> "In fact, a healthy openness never threatens one's own identity. A living culture, enriched by elements from other places, does not import a mere carbon copy of those new elements, but integrates them in its own unique way. The result is a new synthesis that is ultimately beneficial to all, since the original culture itself ends up being nourished" (no. 148).

149. For a healthy relationship between love of one's native land and a sound sense of belonging to our larger human family, it is helpful to keep in mind that global society is not the sum total of different countries, but rather the communion that exists among them. The mutual sense of belonging is prior to the emergence of individual groups. Each particular group becomes part of the fabric of universal communion and there discovers its own beauty. All individuals, whatever their origin, know that they are part of the greater human family, without which they will not be able to understand themselves fully.

150. To see things in this way brings the joyful realization that no one people, culture or individual can achieve everything on its own: to attain fulfilment in life we need others. An awareness of our own limitations and incompleteness, far from being a threat, becomes the key to envisaging and pursuing a common project. For "man is a limited being who is himself limitless."[130]

129. Post-Synodal Apostolic Exhortation *Querida Amazonia* (2 February 2020), 37.

130. Georg Simmel, *Brücke und Tür. Essays des Philosophen zur Geschichte, Religion, Kunst und Gesellschaft*, ed. Michael Landmann, Köhler-Verlag, Stuttgart, 1957, 6.

> "To see things in this way brings the joyful realization that no one people, culture or individual can achieve everything on its own: to attain fulfilment in life we need others. An awareness of our own limitations and incompleteness, far from being a threat, becomes the key to envisaging and pursuing a common project" (no. 150).

Starting with our own region

151. Thanks to regional exchanges, by which poorer countries become open to the wider world, universality does not necessarily water down their distinct features. An appropriate and authentic openness to the world presupposes the capacity to be open to one's neighbour within a family of nations. Cultural, economic and political integration with neighbouring peoples should therefore be accompanied by a process of education that promotes the value of love for one's neighbour, the first indispensable step towards attaining a healthy universal integration.

152. In some areas of our cities, there is still a lively sense of neighbourhood. Each person quite spontaneously perceives a duty to accompany and help his or her neighbour. In places where these community values are maintained, people experience a closeness marked by gratitude, solidarity and reciprocity. The neighbourhood gives them a sense of shared identity.[131] Would that neighbouring countries were able to encourage a similar neighbourly spirit between their peoples! Yet the spirit of individualism also affects relations between countries. The danger of thinking that we have to protect ourselves from one another, of viewing others as competitors or dangerous enemies, also affects relations between peoples in the same region. Perhaps we were trained in this kind of fear and mistrust.

131. Cf. Jaime Hoyos-Vásquez, S.J., "Lógica de las relaciones sociales. Reflexión onto-lógica," *Revista Universitas Philosophica*, 15–16 (December 1990–June 1991), Bogotá, 95–106.

153. There are powerful countries and large businesses that profit from this isolation and prefer to negotiate with each country separately. On the other hand, small or poor countries can sign agreements with their regional neighbours that will allow them to negotiate as a bloc and thus avoid being cut off, isolated and dependent on the great powers. Today, no state can ensure the common good of its population if it remains isolated.

QUESTIONS FOR REFLECTION AND DISCUSSION

1. Pope Francis writes, "When we open our hearts to those who are different, this enables them, while continuing to be themselves, to develop in new ways" (no. 134). Can you think of a time in your life when someone opened their heart to you? What difference did it make for you—in that moment and since then? Can you describe when you opened your heart to someone else, and the affect it produced? Is this evidence for the "joyful realization" (no. 150) of what we have to offer and receive from others? What about a time when you might have missed an opportunity to extend or receive an open heart? What wisdom can you glean from these reflections, in thinking about how you might be able to live even more intentionally with an open heart in looking to the future?
2. In paragraph 140, the pope critiques utilitarian exchanges ordered to self-interest, the tit-for-tat calculations that can encourage people to be guarded or tightfisted. How do you think this stinginess appears to God, who makes the "sun rise on the evil and on the good, and sends rain on the righteous and on the unrighteous" (Matt 5:45)? What are ways you can cultivate a discipline of gratuitousness in your routines, roles, and relationships—as

well as inspire an effort to encounter others across difference? What would an attitude of gratuitousness make possible that another outlook (perhaps one more oriented toward productivity or efficiency) might not?

3. The principle of subsidiarity is an important tenet of Catholic social teaching, as it reminds us that work for justice should take root at the lowest effective level. Pope Francis portrays subsidiarity as a "leaven" that makes transformation possible (no. 142). What examples of social transformation have you seen in your life? What kinds of beliefs, actions, encounters, and relationships contributed to this change—and resulted from it? What lessons does this offer you to seek and be "leaven," personally and as part of a local community?
4. In this section of the encyclical, we read, "I cannot truly encounter another unless I stand on firm foundations, for it is on the basis of these that I can accept the gift the other brings and in turn offer an authentic gift of my own" (no. 143). In light of rising rates of people experiencing anxiety, depression, and social isolation, how do we create the conditions for people to feel greater comfort and confidence to practice encountering others, even when we cannot guarantee an engaging or meaningful exchange? How is Pope Francis's call to conversion (and to open our hearts to others) a challenge to confront insecurity? He suggests, "Perhaps we were trained in this kind of fear and mistrust" (no. 152); if this is true, then what must we learn *and* unlearn on our own, in our families, schools, churches, places of work, political arenas, and so on?
5. Pope Francis lifts up solidarity as a communion proving to be a sum greater than its parts (no. 149). This results from interactions that produce an authentic blending together, yielding "a new synthesis that is ultimately

beneficial to all" (no. 148). What are the main obstacles to participating this kind of synthesis, as you see it? What are necessary ingredients for getting people to invest in this process of "fruitful exchange"? How can we improve our practice of certain virtues—like courage and compassion, authenticity and vulnerability, patience and perseverance—individually and as part of wider communities? What opportunities do you see in your local community for fostering a culture of reciprocity?

FOR FURTHER READING

Pope, Stephen J. *A Step Along the Way: Models of Christian Service*. Maryknoll, NY: Orbis Books, 2015.

Pramuk, Christopher. *Hope Sings, So Beautiful: Graced Encounters across the Color Line*. Collegeville, MN: Liturgical Press, 2013.

Riccardi, Andrea. *To the Margins: Pope Francis and the Mission of the Church*. Maryknoll, NY: Orbis, 2018.

Smith, Gary. *Radical Compassion: Finding Christ in the Heart of the Poor*. Chicago: Loyola Press, 2002.

Spohn, William C. *Go and Do Likewise: Jesus and Ethics*. New York: Continuum, 2006.

Chapter Five

A BETTER KIND OF POLITICS

SYNOPSIS

When we think of politics, feelings like frustration, anger, and cynicism might come to the surface. In moving from theological reflection on solidarity to a pastoral response that puts solidarity into practice, we have to fight the temptation to presume the outcome will only lead to further distrust, disillusionment, or deadlock. We also have to resist any compulsion to privatize religion or restrict it from public relevance. God is the God of life, whose signature deed is liberation (Exod 2:23—3:20; Luke 4:16–21). Christian discipleship is necessarily a political act because it takes responsibility for both promoting human dignity, rights, and responsibilities for the common good as well as dismantling any form of dehumanization, exclusion, or oppression. The separation of church and state prevents any undue influence between these institutions on the other, and also provides a critical distance between them in order for the church to prophetically announce what leads to human flourishing and denounce any and all obstacles to the life in abundance that Jesus came to bring us (John 10:10). If Christians stand on the sidelines of political involvement, they are complicit with an unjust status quo, surrendering their free will to make change possible. The "political" dimension of discipleship cannot be reduced to voting once every four years; loving our neighbors, living the Beatitudes, and practicing the works of mercy imply a spirituality expressed through direct action and long-term social transformation for justice. While faith, hope, and love imply political responsibilities, they should not be partisan, lest our voice and votes become co-opted for narrow interests that keep us from striving for the common good.

When Pope Francis appeals to a "better kind of politics" (no. 154), he envisions this as an essential expression of discipleship as civic duty and the church's mission to be a sacrament, herald, and servant to society in practicing love of neighbor. For this reason, any sufficient pastoral response must involve political action across the individual, interpersonal, and institutional levels of the church. There is no option for neutrality, since any ambivalence only serves to protect the interests of the powerful, never the powerless. Pope Francis does not present the church or Catholic social teaching as a "third way" between conservativism or progressivism, or between individualism and collectivism. Rather, he continues the tradition established by his predecessors to critique ideologies on both the right and left, pointing to failures to adequately defend human dignity, deliver on rights and responsibilities, and build inclusive coalitions to promote the common good. The church's role is to repeat Jesus's call to conversion, to sharpen "our ability to see the need for a change of heart, attitudes and lifestyles. Otherwise, political propaganda, the media and the shapers of public opinion will continue to promote an individualistic and uncritical culture subservient to unregulated economic interests and societal institutions at the service of those who already enjoy too much power" (no. 166). The ongoing work of conversion helps us contend with the impulse of "concupiscence," the "human inclination to be concerned only with myself, my group, my own petty interests" (no. 166). Pope Francis calls for political engagement informed both by views from the vulnerable (no. 155) and with a gaze fixed on "the long-term common good" (no. 178). Ranging from the local to the regional to the national to the international (including the United Nations; see no. 173), political responsibility carries a longitudinal dimension, an obligation to be good stewards of our resources, which are on loan to us from future generations (no. 178). Pope Paul VI claimed, "If you want peace, work for justice." Pope Francis updates this so peace and justice contribute to and draw from an authentic intergenerational solidarity.

In an extended reflection through paragraphs 180–92, the pope underscores that political activity is part of how individual disciples and the church—as both a local and universal reality—love our neighbor as our self. Politics are not in service to the market economy (no. 168); neither are they reserved for career politicians, for everyone is called to build a "civilization of love" (no. 183). This requires consistent political engagement: discipleship ought to inform the way we stay up-to-date about politics at the local and national levels, how we use our power as an ally for the underrepresented, and partner with others to leverage our voices in holding our elected officials accountable to the common good. Politics combines love and justice so that each person is given what is due to them (no. 171) and integrated into the community as participants (no. 187). Politics informed by an ethic of love is inclusive (no. 190), rooted in tenderness that "draws near" to others, to be touched by "the smallest, the weakest, and the poorest" (no. 194). It reorients our vision from measuring results, productivity, or efficiency to what can't be quantified: the change produced by loving and being loved in authentic trust, reciprocal respect, and mutual empowerment. With the long view in mind, we believe in "the hidden power of the seeds of goodness we sow, and thus to initiate processes whose fruits will be reaped by others" (no. 196). We place our hope in the power of love—not the love of power—and the open future it makes possible.

In the final paragraph (no. 197), Pope Francis provides seven questions that serve as an examination of conscience. As we look at our political engagement—the issues we fight for, the problems we work to solve, the advocacy organizations we support, the way we lift our voice to our elected representatives, and how we vote and for whom—we should ask ourselves,

- "How much love did I put into my work?"
- "What did I do for the progress of our people?"
- "What mark did I leave on the life of society?"
- "What real bonds did I create?"
- "What positive forces did I unleash?"
- "How much social peace did I sow?"
- "What good did I achieve in the position that was entrusted to me?"

---

154. The development of a global community of fraternity based on the practice of social friendship on the part of peoples and nations calls for a better kind of politics, one truly at the service of the common good. Sadly, politics today often takes forms that hinder progress towards a different world.

FORMS OF POPULISM AND LIBERALISM

155. Lack of concern for the vulnerable can hide behind a populism that exploits them demagogically for its own purposes, or a liberalism that serves the economic interests of the powerful.

In both cases, it becomes difficult to envisage an open world that makes room for everyone, including the most vulnerable, and shows respect for different cultures.

Popular vs. populist

156. In recent years, the words "populism" and "populist" have invaded the communications media and everyday conversation. As a result, they have lost whatever value they might have had, and have become another source of polarization in an already divided society. Efforts are made to classify entire peoples, groups, societies and governments as "populist" or not. Nowadays it has become impossible for someone to express a view on any subject without being categorized one way or the other, either to be unfairly discredited or to be praised to the skies.

157. The attempt to see populism as a key for interpreting social reality is problematic in another way: it disregards the legitimate meaning of the word "people." Any effort to remove this concept from common parlance could lead to the elimination of the very notion of democracy as "government by the people." If we wish to maintain that society is more than a mere aggregate of individuals, the term "people" proves necessary. There are social phenomena that create majorities, as well as megatrends and communitarian aspirations. Men and women are capable of coming up with shared goals that transcend their differences and can thus engage in a common endeavour. Then too, it is extremely difficult to carry out a long-term project unless it becomes a collective aspiration. All these factors lie behind our use of the words "people" and "popular." Unless they are taken into account—together with a sound critique of demagoguery—a fundamental aspect of social reality would be overlooked.

158. Here, there can be a misunderstanding. "'People' is not a logical category, nor is it a mystical category, if by that we mean that everything the people does is good, or that the people is an 'angelic' reality. Rather, it is a mythic category... When you have to explain what you mean by people, you use logical

categories for the sake of explanation, and necessarily so. Yet in that way you cannot explain what it means to belong to a people. The word 'people' has a deeper meaning that cannot be set forth in purely logical terms. To be part of a people is to be part of a shared identity arising from social and cultural bonds. And that is not something automatic, but rather a slow, difficult process... of advancing towards a common project."[132]

159. "Popular" leaders, those capable of interpreting the feelings and cultural dynamics of a people, and significant trends in society, do exist. The service they provide by their efforts to unite and lead can become the basis of an enduring vision of transformation and growth that would also include making room for others in the pursuit of the common good. But this can degenerate into an unhealthy "populism" when individuals are able to exploit politically a people's culture, under whatever ideological banner, for their own personal advantage or continuing grip on power. Or when, at other times, they seek popularity by appealing to the basest and most selfish inclinations of certain sectors of the population. This becomes all the more serious when, whether in cruder or more subtle forms, it leads to the usurpation of institutions and laws.

160. Closed populist groups distort the word "people," since they are not talking about a true people. The concept of "people" is in fact open-ended. A living and dynamic people, a people with a future, is one constantly open to a new synthesis through its ability to welcome differences. In this way, it does not deny its proper identity, but is open to being mobilized, challenged, broadened and enriched by others, and thus to further growth and development.

161. Another sign of the decline of popular leadership is concern for short-term advantage. One meets popular demands for the sake of gaining votes or support, but without advancing in

---

132. Antonio Spadaro, S.J., *Le orme di un pastore. Una conversazione con Papa Francesco*, in Jorge Mario Bergolio – Papa Francesco, *Nei tuoi occhi è la mia parola. Omelie e discorsi di Buenos Aires 1999–2013*, Rizzoli, Milan 2016, xvi; cf. Apostolic Exhortation *Evangelii Gaudium* (24 November 2013), 220–221: AAS 105 (2013), 1110–1111.

an arduous and constant effort to generate the resources people need to develop and earn a living by their own efforts and creativity. In this regard, I have made it clear that "I have no intention of proposing an irresponsible populism."[133] Eliminating inequality requires an economic growth that can help to tap each region's potential and thus guarantee a sustainable equality.[134] At the same time, it follows that "welfare projects, which meet certain urgent needs, should be considered merely temporary responses."[135]

162. The biggest issue is employment. The truly "popular" thing—since it promotes the good of the people—is to provide everyone with the opportunity to nurture the seeds that God has planted in each of us: our talents, our initiative and our innate resources. This is the finest help we can give to the poor, the best path to a life of dignity. Hence my insistence that, "helping the poor financially must always be a provisional solution in the face of pressing needs. The broader objective should always be to allow them a dignified life through work."[136] Since production systems may change, political systems must keep working to structure society in such a way that everyone has a chance to contribute his or her own talents and efforts. For "there is no poverty worse than that which takes away work and the dignity of work."[137] In a genuinely developed society, work is an essential dimension of social life, for it is not only a means of earning one's daily bread, but also of personal growth, the building of healthy relationships, self-expression and the exchange of gifts. Work gives us a sense of shared responsibility for the development of the world, and ultimately, for our life as a people.

---

133. Apostolic Exaltation *Evangelii Gaudium* (24 November 2013), 204: AAS 105 (2013), 1106.

134. Cf. ibid.: AAS 105 (2013), 1105–1106.

135. Ibid., 202: AAS 105 (2013), 1105.

136. Encyclical Letter *Laudato Si'* (24 May 2015), 128: AAS 107 (2015), 898.

137. *Address to the Diplomatic Corps Accredited to the Holy See* (12 January 2015): AAS 107 (2015), 165; cf. *Address to Participants in the World Meeting of Popular Movements* (28 October 2014): AAS 106 (2014), 851–859.

The benefits and limits of liberal approaches

163. The concept of a "people," which naturally entails a positive view of community and cultural bonds, is usually rejected by individualistic liberal approaches, which view society as merely the sum of coexisting interests. One speaks of respect for freedom, but without roots in a shared narrative; in certain contexts, those who defend the rights of the most vulnerable members of society tend to be criticized as populists. The notion of a people is considered an abstract construct, something that does not really exist. But this is to create a needless dichotomy. Neither the notion of "people" nor that of "neighbour" can be considered purely abstract or romantic, in such a way that social organization, science and civic institutions can be rejected or treated with contempt.[138]

164. Charity, on the other hand, unites both dimensions—the abstract and the institutional—since it calls for an effective process of historical change that embraces everything: institutions, law, technology, experience, professional expertise, scientific analysis, administrative procedures, and so forth. For that matter, "private life cannot exist unless it is protected by public order. A domestic hearth has no real warmth unless it is safeguarded by law, by a state of tranquillity founded on law, and enjoys a minimum of wellbeing ensured by the division of labour, commercial exchange, social justice and political citizenship."[139]

165. True charity is capable of incorporating all these elements in its concern for others. In the case of personal encounters, including those involving a distant or forgotten brother or sister, it can do so by employing all the resources that the institutions of an organized, free and creative society are capable of generating. Even the Good Samaritan, for example, needed to have a nearby inn that could provide the help that he was personally unable to offer. Love of neighbour is concrete and squanders none of the resources needed to bring about historical change

---

138. A similar point could be made with regard to the biblical category of the Kingdom of God.

139. Paul Ricoeur, *Histoire et Verité*, ed. Le Seuil Paris, 1967, 122.

that can benefit the poor and disadvantaged. At times, however, leftist ideologies or social doctrines linked to individualistic ways of acting and ineffective procedures affect only a few, while the majority of those left behind remain dependent on the goodwill of others. This demonstrates the need for a greater spirit of fraternity, but also a more efficient worldwide organization to help resolve the problems plaguing the abandoned who are suffering and dying in poor countries. It also shows that there is no one solution, no single acceptable methodology, no economic recipe that can be applied indiscriminately to all. Even the most rigorous scientific studies can propose different courses of action.

166. Everything, then, depends on our ability to see the need for a change of heart, attitudes and lifestyles. Otherwise, political propaganda, the media and the shapers of public opinion will continue to promote an individualistic and uncritical culture subservient to unregulated economic interests and societal institutions at the service of those who already enjoy too much power. My criticism of the technocratic paradigm involves more than simply thinking that if we control its excesses everything will be fine. The bigger risk does not come from specific objects, material realities or institutions, but from the way that they are used. It has to do with human weakness, the proclivity to selfishness that is part of what the Christian tradition refers to as "concupiscence": the human inclination to be concerned only with myself, my group, my own petty interests. Concupiscence is not a flaw limited to our own day. It has been present from the beginning of humanity, and has simply changed and taken on different forms down the ages, using whatever means each moment of history can provide. Concupiscence, however, can be overcome with the help of God.

167. Education and upbringing, concern for others, a well-integrated view of life and spiritual growth: all these are essential for quality human relationships and for enabling society itself to react against injustices, aberrations and abuses of economic, technological, political and media power. Some liberal approaches ignore this factor of human weakness; they envisage a world that

follows a determined order and is capable by itself of ensuring a bright future and providing solutions for every problem.

> "Education and upbringing, concern for others, a well-integrated view of life and spiritual growth: all these are essential for quality human relationships and for enabling society itself to react against injustices, aberrations and abuses of economic, technological, political and media power. Some liberal approaches ignore this factor of human weakness; they envisage a world that follows a determined order and is capable by itself of ensuring a bright future and providing solutions for every problem. The marketplace, by itself, cannot resolve every problem, however much we are asked to believe this dogma of neoliberal faith. Whatever the challenge, this impoverished and repetitive school of thought always offers the same recipes. Neoliberalism simply reproduces itself by resorting to the magic theories of 'spillover' or 'trickle'—without using the name—as the only solution to societal problems. There is little appreciation of the fact that the alleged 'spillover' does not resolve the inequality that gives rise to new forms of violence threatening the fabric of society. It is imperative to have a proactive economic policy directed at 'promoting an economy that favors productive diversity and business creativity' and makes it possible for jobs to be created and not cut" (nos. 167–68).

168. The marketplace, by itself, cannot resolve every problem, however much we are asked to believe this dogma of neoliberal faith. Whatever the challenge, this impoverished and repetitive school of thought always offers the same recipes. Neoliberalism simply reproduces itself by resorting to the magic

theories of "spillover" or "trickle"—without using the name—as the only solution to societal problems. There is little appreciation of the fact that the alleged "spillover" does not resolve the inequality that gives rise to new forms of violence threatening the fabric of society. It is imperative to have a proactive economic policy directed at "promoting an economy that favours productive diversity and business creativity"[140] and makes it possible for jobs to be created and not cut. Financial speculation fundamentally aimed at quick profit continues to wreak havoc. Indeed, "without internal forms of solidarity and mutual trust, the market cannot completely fulfil its proper economic function. And today this trust has ceased to exist."[141] The story did not end the way it was meant to, and the dogmatic formulae of prevailing economic theory proved not to be infallible. The fragility of world systems in the face of the pandemic has demonstrated that not everything can be resolved by market freedom. It has also shown that, in addition to recovering a sound political life that is not subject to the dictates of finance, "we must put human dignity back at the centre and on that pillar build the alternative social structures we need."[142]

169. In some closed and monochrome economic approaches, for example, there seems to be no place for popular movements that unite the unemployed, temporary and informal workers and many others who do not easily find a place in existing structures. Yet those movements manage various forms of popular economy and of community production. What is needed is a model of social, political and economic participation "that can include popular movements and invigorate local, national and international governing structures with that torrent of moral energy that springs from including the excluded in the building of a common destiny," while also ensuring that "these experiences of solidarity which grow up from below, from the subsoil of the planet—

---

140. Encyclical Letter *Laudato Si'* (24 May 2015), 129: AAS 107 (2015), 899.

141. Benedict XVI, Encyclical Letter *Caritas in Veritate* (29 June 2009), 35: AAS 101 (2009), 670.

142. *Address to Participants in the World Meeting of Popular Movements* (28 October 2014): AAS 106 (2014), 858.

can come together, be more coordinated, keep on meeting one another."[143] This, however, must happen in a way that will not betray their distinctive way of acting as "sowers of change, promoters of a process involving millions of actions, great and small, creatively intertwined like words in a poem."[144] In that sense, such movements are "social poets" that, in their own way, work, propose, promote and liberate. They help make possible an integral human development that goes beyond "the idea of social policies being a policy *for* the poor, but never *with* the poor and never *of* the poor, much less part of a project that reunites peoples."[145] They may be troublesome, and certain "theorists" may find it hard to classify them, yet we must find the courage to acknowledge that, without them, "democracy atrophies, turns into a mere word, a formality; it loses its representative character and becomes disembodied, since it leaves out the people in their daily struggle for dignity, in the building of their future."[146]

> "What is needed is a model of social, political and economic participation 'that can include popular movements and invigorate local, national and international governing structures with that torrent of moral energy that springs from including the excluded in the building of a common destiny,' while also ensuring that 'these experiences of solidarity which grow up from below, from the subsoil of the planet—can come together, be more coordinated, keep on meeting one another.' This, however, must happen in a way that will not betray their distinctive way of acting as 'sowers of change, promoters of a process involving millions of actions, great and small, creatively intertwined like words in a

143. Ibid.

144. *Address to Participants in the World Meeting of Popular Movements* (5 November 2016): *L'Osservatore Romano*, 7–8 November 2016, pp. 4–5.

145. Ibid.

146. Ibid.

poem.' In that sense, such movements are 'social poets' that, in their own way, work, propose, promote and liberate. They help make possible an integral human development that goes beyond 'the idea of social policies being a policy *for* the poor, but never *with* the poor and never *of* the poor, much less part of a project that reunites peoples'" (no. 169).

INTERNATIONAL POWER

170. I would once more observe that "the financial crisis of 2007–08 provided an opportunity to develop a new economy, more attentive to ethical principles, and new ways of regulating speculative financial practices and virtual wealth. But the response to the crisis did not include rethinking the outdated criteria which continue to rule the world."[147] Indeed, it appears that the actual strategies developed worldwide in the wake of the crisis fostered greater individualism, less integration and increased freedom for the truly powerful, who always find a way to escape unscathed.

171. I would also insist that "to give to each his own—to cite the classic definition of justice—means that no human individual or group can consider itself absolute, entitled to bypass the dignity and the rights of other individuals or their social groupings. The effective distribution of power (especially political, economic, defence-related and technological power) among a plurality of subjects, and the creation of a juridical system for regulating claims and interests, are one concrete way of limiting power. Yet today's world presents us with many false rights and—at the same time—broad sectors which are vulnerable, victims of power badly exercised."[148]

147. Encyclical Letter *Laudato Si'* (24 May 2015), 189. AAS 107 (2015), 922.

148. *Address to the Members of the General Assembly of the United Nations Organization*, New York (25 September 2015): AAS 107 (2015), 1037.

172. The twenty-first century "is witnessing a weakening of the power of nation states, chiefly because the economic and financial sectors, being transnational, tend to prevail over the political. Given this situation, it is essential to devise stronger and more efficiently organized international institutions, with functionaries who are appointed fairly by agreement among national governments, and empowered to impose sanctions."[149] When we talk about the possibility of some form of world authority regulated by law,[150] we need not necessarily think of a personal authority. Still, such an authority ought at least to promote more effective world organizations, equipped with the power to provide for the global common good, the elimination of hunger and poverty and the sure defence of fundamental human rights.

173. In this regard, I would also note the need for a reform of "the United Nations Organization, and likewise of economic institutions and international finance, so that the concept of the family of nations can acquire real teeth."[151] Needless to say, this calls for clear legal limits to avoid power being co-opted only by a few countries and to prevent cultural impositions or a restriction of the basic freedoms of weaker nations on the basis of ideological differences. For "the international community is a juridical community founded on the sovereignty of each member state, without bonds of subordination that deny or limit its independence."[152] At the same time, "the work of the United Nations, according to the principles set forth in the Preamble and the first Articles of its founding Charter, can be seen as the development and promotion of the rule of law, based on the realization that justice is an essential condition for achieving the ideal of universal fraternity... There is a need to ensure the uncontested rule of law and tireless recourse to negotiation, mediation and arbitration, as proposed by the Charter of the United Nations,

149. Encyclical Letter *Laudato Si'* (24 May 2015), 175: AAS 107 (2015), 916–917.

150. Cf. Benedict XVI, Encyclical Letter *Caritas in Veritate* (29 June 2009), 67: AAS 101 (2009), 700–701.

151. Ibid.: AAS 101 (2009), 700.

152. Pontifical Council for Justice and Peace, *Compendium of the Social Doctrine of the Church*, 434.

which constitutes truly a fundamental juridical norm."[153] There is need to prevent this Organization from being delegitimized, since its problems and shortcomings are capable of being jointly addressed and resolved.

174. Courage and generosity are needed in order freely to establish shared goals and to ensure the worldwide observance of certain essential norms. For this to be truly useful, it is essential to uphold "the need to be faithful to agreements undertaken (*pacta sunt servanda*),"[154] and to avoid the "temptation to appeal to the law of force rather than to the force of law."[155] This means reinforcing the "normative instruments for the peaceful resolution of controversies... so as to strengthen their scope and binding force."[156] Among these normative instruments, preference should be given to multilateral agreements between states, because, more than bilateral agreements, they guarantee the promotion of a truly universal common good and the protection of weaker states.

175. Providentially, many groups and organizations within civil society help to compensate for the shortcomings of the international community, its lack of coordination in complex situations, its lack of attention to fundamental human rights and to the critical needs of certain groups. Here we can see a concrete application of the principle of subsidiarity, which justifies the participation and activity of communities and organizations on lower levels as a means of integrating and complementing the activity of the state. These groups and organizations often carry out commendable efforts in the service of the common good and their members at times show true heroism, revealing something of the grandeur of which our humanity is still capable.

153. *Address to the Members of the General Assembly of the United Nations Organization*, New York (25 September 2015): AAS 107 (2015), 1037, 1041.

154. Pontifical Council for Justice and Peace, *Compendium of the Social Doctrine of the Church*, 437.

155. Saint John Paul II, *Message for the 2004 World Day of Peace*, 5: AAS 96 (2004), 117.

156. Pontifical Council for Justice and Peace, *Compendium of the Social Doctrine of the Church*, 439.

SOCIAL AND POLITICAL CHARITY

176. For many people today, politics is a distasteful word, often due to the mistakes, corruption and inefficiency of some politicians. There are also attempts to discredit politics, to replace it with economics or to twist it to one ideology or another. Yet can our world function without politics? Can there be an effective process of growth towards universal fraternity and social peace without a sound political life?[157]

The politics we need

177. Here I would once more observe that "politics must not be subject to the economy, nor should the economy be subject to the dictates of an efficiency-driven paradigm of technocracy."[158] Although misuse of power, corruption, disregard for law and inefficiency must clearly be rejected, "economics without politics cannot be justified, since this would make it impossible to favour other ways of handling the various aspects of the present crisis."[159] Instead, "what is needed is a politics which is far-sighted and capable of a new, integral and interdisciplinary approach to handling the different aspects of the crisis."[160] In other words, a "healthy politics... capable of reforming and coordinating institutions, promoting best practices and overcoming undue pressure and bureaucratic inertia."[161] We cannot expect economics to do this, nor can we allow economics to take over the real power of the state.

178. In the face of many petty forms of politics focused on immediate interests, I would repeat that "true statecraft is manifest when, in difficult times, we uphold high principles and think of the long-term common good. Political powers do not

157. Cf. Social Commission of the Bishops of France, Declaration *Réhabiliter la Politique* (17 February 1999).

158. Encyclical Letter *Laudato Si'* (24 May 2015), 189: AAS 107 (2015), 922.

159. Ibid., 196: AAS 107 (2015), 925.

160. Ibid., 197: AAS 107 (2015), 925.

161. Ibid., 181: AAS 107 (2015), 919.

find it easy to assume this duty in the work of nation-building,"[162] much less in forging a common project for the human family, now and in the future. Thinking of those who will come after us does not serve electoral purposes, yet it is what authentic justice demands. As the Bishops of Portugal have taught, the earth "is lent to each generation, to be handed on to the generation that follows."[163]

179. Global society is suffering from grave structural deficiencies that cannot be resolved by piecemeal solutions or quick fixes. Much needs to change, through fundamental reform and major renewal. Only a healthy politics, involving the most diverse sectors and skills, is capable of overseeing this process. An economy that is an integral part of a political, social, cultural and popular programme directed to the common good could pave the way for "different possibilities which do not involve stifling human creativity and its ideals of progress, but rather directing that energy along new channels."[164]

Political love

180. Recognizing that all people are our brothers and sisters, and seeking forms of social friendship that include everyone, is not merely utopian. It demands a decisive commitment to devising effective means to this end. Any effort along these lines becomes a noble exercise of charity. For whereas individuals can help others in need, when they join together in initiating social processes of fraternity and justice for all, they enter the "field of charity at its most vast, namely political charity."[165] This entails working for a social and political order whose soul is

---

162. Ibid., 178: AAS 107 (2015), 918.

163. Portuguese Bishops' Conference, Pastoral Letter *Responsabilidade Solidária pelo Bem Comum* (15 September 2003), 20; cf. Encyclical Letter *Laudato Si'* (24 May 2015), 159: AAS 107 (2015), 911.

164. Encyclical Letter *Laudato Si'* (24 May 2015), 191: AAS 107 (2015), 923.

165. Pius XI, *Address to the Italian Catholic Federation of University Students* (18 December 1927): *L'Osservatore Romano*, 23 December 1927, p. 3.

social charity.[166] Once more, I appeal for a renewed appreciation of politics as "a lofty vocation and one of the highest forms of charity, inasmuch as it seeks the common good."[167]

181. Every commitment inspired by the Church's social doctrine is "derived from charity, which according to the teaching of Jesus is the synthesis of the entire Law (cf. *Mt* 22:36–40)."[168] This means acknowledging that "love, overflowing with small gestures of mutual care, is also civic and political, and it makes itself felt in every action that seeks to build a better world."[169] For this reason, charity finds expression not only in close and intimate relationships but also in "macro-relationships: social, economic and political."[170]

182. This political charity is born of a social awareness that transcends every individualistic mindset: "'Social charity makes us love the common good,' it makes us effectively seek the good of all people, considered not only as individuals or private persons, but also in the social dimension that unites them."[171] Each of us is fully a person when we are part of a people; at the same time, there are no peoples without respect for the individuality of each person. "People" and "person" are correlative terms. Nonetheless, there are attempts nowadays to reduce persons to isolated individuals easily manipulated by powers pursuing spurious interests. Good politics will seek ways of building communities at every level of social life, in order to recalibrate and reorient globalization and thus avoid its disruptive effects.

---

166. Cf. id., Encyclical Letter *Quadragesimo Anno* (15 May 1931): AAS 23 (1931), 206–207.

167. Apostolic Exhortation *Evangelii Gaudium* (24 November 2013), 205: AAS 105 (2013), 1106.

168. Benedict XVI, Encyclical Letter *Caritas in Veritate* (29 June 2009), 2: AAS 101 (2009), 642.

169. Encyclical Letter Laudato Si' (24 May 2015), 231: AAS 107 (2015), 937.

170. Benedict XVI, Encyclical Letter *Caritas in Veritate* (29 June 2009), 2: AAS 101 (2009), 642.

171. Pontifical Council for Justice and Peace, *Compendium of the Social Doctrine of the Church*, 207.

Effective love

183. "Social love"[172] makes it possible to advance towards a civilization of love, to which all of us can feel called. Charity, with its impulse to universality, is capable of building a new world.[173] No mere sentiment, it is the best means of discovering effective paths of development for everyone. Social love is a "force capable of inspiring new ways of approaching the problems of today's world, of profoundly renewing structures, social organizations and legal systems from within."[174]

> "Charity, with its impulse to universality, is capable of building a new world. No mere sentiment, it is the best means of discovering effective paths of development for everyone. Social love is a 'force capable of inspiring new ways of approaching the problems of today's world, of profoundly renewing structures, social organizations and legal systems from within'" (no. 183).

184. Charity is at the heart of every healthy and open society, yet today "it is easily dismissed as irrelevant for interpreting and giving direction to moral responsibility."[175] Charity, when accompanied by a commitment to the truth, is much more than personal feeling, and consequently need not "fall prey to contingent subjective emotions and opinions."[176] Indeed its close relation to truth fosters its universality and preserves it from being

---

172. Saint John Paul II, Encyclical Letter *Redemptor Hominis* (4 March 1979), 15: AAS 71 (1979), 288.

173. Cf. Saint Paul VI, Encyclical Letter *Populorum Progressio* (26 March 1967), 44: AAS 59 (1967), 279.

174. Pontifical Council for Justice and Peace, *Compendium of the Social Doctrine of the Church*, 207.

175. Benedict XVI, Encyclical Letter *Caritas in Veritate* (29 June 2009), 2: AAS 101 (2009), 642.

176. Ibid., 3: AAS 101 (2009), 643.

"confined to a narrow field devoid of relationships."[177] Otherwise, it would be "excluded from the plans and processes of promoting human development of universal range, in dialogue between knowledge and praxis.[178] Without truth, emotion lacks relational and social content. Charity's openness to truth thus protects it from "a fideism that deprives it of its human and universal breadth."[179]

185. Charity needs the light of the truth that we constantly seek. "That light is both the light of reason and the light of faith,"[180] and does not admit any form of relativism. Yet it also respects the development of the sciences and their essential contribution to finding the surest and most practical means of achieving the desired results. For when the good of others is at stake, good intentions are not enough. Concrete efforts must be made to bring about whatever they and their nations need for the sake of their development.

THE EXERCISE OF POLITICAL LOVE

186. There is a kind of love that is "elicited": its acts proceed directly from the virtue of charity and are directed to individuals and peoples. There is also a "commanded" love, expressed in those acts of charity that spur people to create more sound institutions, more just regulations, more supportive structures.[181] It follows that "it is an equally indispensable act of love to strive to organize and structure society so that one's neighbour will not find himself in poverty."[182] It is an act of charity to assist someone

177. Ibid., 4: AAS 101 (2009), 643.

178. Ibid.

179. Ibid., 3: AAS 101 (2009), 643.

180. Ibid.: AAS 101 (2009), 642.

181. Catholic moral doctrine, following the teaching of Saint Thomas Aquinas, distinguishes between "elicited" and "commanded" acts; cf. *Summa Theologiae*, I–II, qq. 8–17; M. Zalba, S.J., *Theologiae Moralis Summa. Theologia Moralis Fundamentalis. Tractatus de Virtutibus Theologicis*, ed. BAC, Madrid, 1952, vol. I, 69; A. Royo Marín, *Teología de la Perfección Cristiana*, ed. BAC, Madrid, 1962, 192–196.

182. Pontifical Council for Justice and Peace, *Compendium of the Social Doctrine of the Church*, 208.

suffering, but it is also an act of charity, even if we do not know that person, to work to change the social conditions that caused his or her suffering. If someone helps an elderly person cross a river, that is a fine act of charity. The politician, on the other hand, builds a bridge, and that too is an act of charity. While one person can help another by providing something to eat, the politician creates a job for that other person, and thus practices a lofty form of charity that ennobles his or her political activity.

Sacrifices born of love

187. This charity, which is the spiritual heart of politics, is always a preferential love shown to those in greatest need; it undergirds everything we do on their behalf.[183] Only a gaze transformed by charity can enable the dignity of others to be recognized and, as a consequence, the poor to be acknowledged and valued in their dignity, respected in their identity and culture, and thus truly integrated into society. That gaze is at the heart of the authentic spirit of politics. It sees paths open up that are different from those of a soulless pragmatism. It makes us realize that "the scandal of poverty cannot be addressed by promoting strategies of containment that only tranquilize the poor and render them tame and inoffensive. How sad it is when we find, behind allegedly altruistic works, the other being reduced to passivity."[184] What are needed are new pathways of self-expression and participation in society. Education serves these by making it possible for each human being to shape his or her own future. Here too we see the importance of the principle of *subsidiarity*, which is inseparable from the principle of *solidarity*.

188. These considerations help us recognize the urgent need to combat all that threatens or violates fundamental human rights. Politicians are called to "tend to the needs of

---

183. Cf. Saint John Paul II, Encyclical Letter *Sollicitudo Rei Socialis* (30 December 1987), 42: AAS 80 (1988), 572–574; Encyclical Letter *Centesimus Annus* (1 May 1991), 11: AAS 83 (1991), 806–807.

184. *Address to Participants in the World Meeting of Popular Movements* (28 October 2014): AAS 106 (2014), 852.

individuals and peoples. To tend those in need takes strength and tenderness, effort and generosity in the midst of a functionalistic and privatized mindset that inexorably leads to a 'throwaway culture'… It involves taking responsibility for the present with its situations of utter marginalization and anguish, and being capable of bestowing dignity upon it."[185] It will likewise inspire intense efforts to ensure that "everything be done to protect the status and dignity of the human person."[186] Politicians are doers, builders with ambitious goals, possessed of a broad, realistic and pragmatic gaze that looks beyond their own borders. Their biggest concern should not be about a drop in the polls, but about finding effective solutions to "the phenomenon of social and economic exclusion, with its baneful consequences: human trafficking, the marketing of human organs and tissues, the sexual exploitation of boys and girls, slave labour, including prostitution, the drug and weapons trade, terrorism and international organized crime. Such is the magnitude of these situations, and their toll in innocent lives, that we must avoid every temptation to fall into a declarationist nominalism that would assuage our consciences. We need to ensure that our institutions are truly effective in the struggle against all these scourges."[187] This includes taking intelligent advantage of the immense resources offered by technological development.

> "'To tend those in need takes strength and tenderness, effort and generosity in the midst of a functionalistic and privatized mindset that inexorably leads to a "throwaway culture"… It involves taking responsibility for the present with its situations of utter marginalization and anguish, and being capable of bestowing dignity upon

185. *Address to the European Parliament*, Strasbourg (25 November 2014): AAS 106 (2014), 999.

186. *Address at the Meeting with Authorities and the Diplomatic Corps in the Central African Republic*, Bangui (29 November 2015): AAS 107 (2015), 1320.

187. *Address to the United Nations Organization*, New York (25 September 2015): AAS 107 (2015), 1039.

it.' It will likewise inspire intense efforts to ensure that 'everything be done to protect the status and dignity of the human person.' Politicians are doers, builders with ambitious goals, possessed of a broad, realistic and pragmatic gaze that looks beyond their own borders. Their biggest concern should not be about a drop in the polls, but about finding effective solutions to 'the phenomenon of social and economic exclusion, with its baneful consequences: human trafficking, the marketing of human organs and tissues, the sexual exploitation of boys and girls, slave labor, including prostitution, the drug and weapons trade, terrorism and international organized crime. Such is the magnitude of these situations, and their toll in innocent lives, that we must avoid every temptation to fall into a declarationist nominalism that would assuage our consciences'" (no. 188).

189. We are still far from a globalization of the most basic of human rights. That is why world politics needs to make the effective elimination of hunger one of its foremost and imperative goals. Indeed, "when financial speculation manipulates the price of food, treating it as just another commodity, millions of people suffer and die from hunger. At the same time, tons of food are thrown away. This constitutes a genuine scandal. Hunger is criminal; food is an inalienable right."[188] Often, as we carry on our semantic or ideological disputes, we allow our brothers and sisters to die of hunger and thirst, without shelter or access to health care. Alongside these basic needs that remain unmet, trafficking in persons represents another source of shame for humanity, one that international politics, moving beyond fine speeches

188. *Address to Participants in the World Meeting of Popular Movements* (28 October 2014): AAS 106 (2014), 853.

and good intentions, must no longer tolerate. These things are essential; they can no longer be deferred.

A love that integrates and unites

190. Political charity is also expressed in a spirit of openness to everyone. Government leaders should be the first to make the sacrifices that foster encounter and to seek convergence on at least some issues. They should be ready to listen to other points of view and to make room for everyone. Through sacrifice and patience, they can help to create a beautiful polyhedral reality in which everyone has a place. Here, economic negotiations do not work. Something else is required: an exchange of gifts for the common good. It may seem naïve and utopian, yet we cannot renounce this lofty aim.

191. At a time when various forms of fundamentalist intolerance are damaging relationships between individuals, groups and peoples, let us be committed to living and teaching the value of respect for others, a love capable of welcoming differences, and the priority of the dignity of every human being over his or her ideas, opinions, practices and even sins. Even as forms of fanaticism, closedmindedness and social and cultural fragmentation proliferate in present-day society, a good politician will take the first step and insist that different voices be heard. Disagreements may well give rise to conflicts, but uniformity proves stifling and leads to cultural decay. May we not be content with being enclosed in one fragment of reality.

192. In this regard, Grand Imam Ahmad Al-Tayyeb and I have called upon "the architects of international policy and world economy to work strenuously to spread the culture of tolerance and of living together in peace; to intervene at the earliest opportunity to stop the shedding of innocent blood."[189] When a specific policy sows hatred and fear towards other nations in the name of

189. *Document on Human Fraternity for World Peace and Living Together*, Abu Dhabi (4 February 2019): *L'Osservatore Romano*, 4–5 February 2019, p. 6.

its own country's welfare, there is need to be concerned, to react in time and immediately to correct the course.

FRUITFULNESS OVER RESULTS

193. Apart from their tireless activity, politicians are also men and women. They are called to practice love in their daily interpersonal relationships. As persons, they need to consider that "the modern world, with its technical advances, tends increasingly to functionalize the satisfaction of human desires, now classified and subdivided among different services. Less and less will people be called by name, less and less will this unique being be treated as a person with his or her own feelings, sufferings, problems, joys and family. Their illnesses will be known only in order to cure them, their financial needs only to provide for them, their lack of a home only to give them lodging, their desires for recreation and entertainment only to satisfy them." Yet it must never be forgotten that "loving the most insignificant of human beings as a brother, as if there were no one else in the world but him, cannot be considered a waste of time."[190]

194. Politics too must make room for a tender love of others. "What is tenderness? It is love that draws near and becomes real. A movement that starts from our heart and reaches the eyes, the ears and the hands... Tenderness is the path of choice for the strongest, most courageous men and women."[191] Amid the daily concerns of political life, "the smallest, the weakest, the poorest should touch our hearts: indeed, they have a 'right' to appeal to our heart and soul. They are our brothers and sisters, and as such we must love and care for them."[192]

---

190. René Voillaume, *Frères de tous*, ed. Cerf, Paris, 1968, 12–13.

191. *Video Message to the TED Conference in Vancouver* (26 April 2017): 27 April 2017, p. 7.

192. *General Audience* (18 February 2015): *L'Osservatore Romano*, 19 February 2015, p. 8.

> "Politics too must make room for a tender love of others. 'What is tenderness? It is love that draws near and becomes real. A movement that starts from our heart and reaches the eyes, the ears and the hands... Tenderness is the path of choice for the strongest, most courageous men and women.' Amid the daily concerns of political life, 'the smallest, the weakest, the poorest should touch our hearts: indeed, they have a "right" to appeal to our heart and soul. They are our brothers and sisters, and as such we must love and care for them'" (no. 194).

195. All this can help us realize that what is important is not constantly achieving great results, since these are not always possible. In political activity, we should remember that, "appearances notwithstanding, every person is immensely holy and deserves our love. Consequently, if I can help at least one person to have a better life, that already justifies the offering of my life. It is a wonderful thing to be God's faithful people. We achieve fulfilment when we break down walls and our hearts are filled with faces and names!"[193] The great goals of our dreams and plans may only be achieved in part. Yet beyond this, those who love, and who no longer view politics merely as a quest for power, "may be sure that none of our acts of love will be lost, nor any of our acts of sincere concern for others. No single act of love for God will be lost, no generous effort is meaningless, no painful endurance is wasted. All of these encircle our world like a vital force."[194]

196. For this reason, it is truly noble to place our hope in the hidden power of the seeds of goodness we sow, and thus to initiate processes whose fruits will be reaped by others. Good politics combines love with hope and with confidence in the reserves of goodness present in human hearts. Indeed, "authentic political

193. Apostolic Exhortation *Evangelii Gaudium* (24 November 2013), 274: AAS 105 (2013), 1130.

194. Ibid., 279: AAS 105 (2013), 1132.

life, built upon respect for law and frank dialogue between individuals, is constantly renewed whenever there is a realization that every woman and man, and every new generation, brings the promise of new relational, intellectual, cultural and spiritual energies."[195]

197. Viewed in this way, politics is something more noble than posturing, marketing and media spin. These sow nothing but division, conflict and a bleak cynicism incapable of mobilizing people to pursue a common goal. At times, in thinking of the future, we do well to ask ourselves, "Why I am doing this?", "What is my real aim?" For as time goes on, reflecting on the past, the questions will not be: "How many people endorsed me?", "How many voted for me?", "How many had a positive image of me?" The real, and potentially painful, questions will be, "How much love did I put into my work?" "What did I do for the progress of our people?" "What mark did I leave on the life of society?" "What real bonds did I create?" "What positive forces did I unleash?" "How much social peace did I sow?" "What good did I achieve in the position that was entrusted to me?"

QUESTIONS FOR REFLECTION AND DISCUSSION

1. Pope Francis dedicates several paragraphs to a critique of populism as "another source of polarization" (no. 156ff.). As you reflect and pray with this document, how are you coming to see the role of the church as a social critic? How can faith address the secularism and moral relativism on the left and the free-market economics and unchecked individualism on the right? How can the church inspire a politics that resists special interests

195. *Message for the 2019 World Day of Peace* (8 December 2018), 5: *L'Osservatore Romano*, 19 December 2018, p. 8.

and works to "guarantee a sustainable equality" (no. 161)?

2. Politics is about linking individuals to systems and structures. Pope Francis observes that "even the Good Samaritan, for example, needed to have a nearby inn that could provide the help that he was personally unable to offer. Love of neighbour is concrete and squanders none of the resources needed to bring about historical change that can benefit the poor and disadvantaged" (no. 165). What existing relationships, networks, and organizations can be leveraged to bridge serving persons in need with the long-term structural reforms? As the saying goes, "Prevention is the best cure." How can you (and your faith community) turn more attention to preventing dehumanization and deprivation, exploitation and exclusion on the local, regional, and national levels—and beyond?
3. Pope Francis contests politics in service to economics because an economic lens risks sacrificing human (and environmental) well-being for the sake of maximizing efficiency or increasing revenue (no. 168). In the face of so many concerns about scarce resources, market competition, and other financial interests or constraints, how can you avoid being swallowed by economic insecurity? What would it take for Christians to advance a vision of personal and collective flourishing as more essential than a "healthy bottom line"?
4. How do you respond to the pope's presentation of love as necessarily political? Pope Francis claims, "Recognizing that all people are our brothers and sisters, and seeking forms of social friendship that include everyone, is not merely utopian. It demands a decisive commitment to devising effective means to this end. Any effort along these lines becomes a noble exercise of charity" (no. 180). How does this part of *Fratelli Tutti* encourage and

challenge you to stretch your political muscle, lift your voice, and invite others to join you in political action as a work of love? In the face of so much political disillusionment, disenfranchisement, and corruption, how does this encyclical invite you to reconsider what the power of love makes possible?

5. Pope Francis addresses politicians as ambitious and hardworking visionaries (no. 188). Too often, however, politics devolves into a partisan game of tug-of-war, where compromise becomes a dirty word. It may be easy to demonize politicians and members of the "other" party. This also makes it convenient to blame our community or country's problems on our elected officials. What role can Christian individuals and communities play in reducing polarization? Improving transparency and accountability? Endorsing bipartisan collaboration? St. Augustine describes the virtuous community as a diverse collection of individuals united not by common interests, but shared objects of love.* How can our faith inspire a more inclusive, equitable, and interdependent approach to politics in service to the shared objects of our love?

FOR FURTHER READING

Cafardi, Nicholas P., ed. *Voting and Faithfulness: Catholic Perspectives on Politics*. Mahwah, NJ: Paulist Press, 2020.

Eggemeier, Matthew T., and Peter Joseph Fritz. *The Politics of Mercy: Catholic Life in an Era of Inequality, Racism, and Violence*. New York: Herder & Herder, 2020.

* See, e.g., Augustine, *City of God*, 19.24.

Heyer, Kristin E. *Prophetic & Public: The Social Witness of U.S. Catholicism*. Washington, DC: Georgetown University Press, 2006.

Kavanaugh, John F. *Following Christ in a Consumer Society*. Maryknoll, NY: Orbis Books, 2006.

Rubio, Julie Hanlon. *Hope for Common Ground: Mediating the Personal and the Political in a Divided Church*. Washington, DC: Georgetown University Press, 2016.

Chapter Six

DIALOGUE AND FRIENDSHIP IN SOCIETY

SYNOPSIS

"If we want to encounter and help one another, we have to dialogue," Pope Francis insists (no. 198). Dialogue may seem like an obvious dimension of the "culture of encounter" he has championed throughout his pontificate, but it nevertheless remains all too rare. Often our interpersonal exchanges reveal people speaking past each other, not actually listening to the other person or trying to understand the truth they are voicing. Dialogue is only possible when we are fully present and prepared to listen, even when we are tempted to be distracted or are faced with the possibility of hearing something uncomfortable. The act of listening to another person shows them that they have something worthy to offer others and be received by others (no. 203). Genuine dialogue leaves people changed because it helps us see reality from a perspective other than our own. Every encounter expands access to more vantage points, cultivates empathy, broadens our understanding of reality, and deepens our relationships. Pope Francis uses the image of a polyhedron to show the multifaceted dimensions of catholicity—a unity in diversity—that emerges from practicing a "culture of encounter" as an indispensable step in the journey toward peace making and realizing a culture of solidarity (nos. 215–17).

Pope Francis reminds us that dialogue is different than debate or the harsh interactions we typically see in media and online. He attests, "The heroes of the future will be those who can break with this unhealthy mindset and determine respectfully to promote truthfulness, aside from personal interest" (no. 202). Authentic dialogue begins without expecting everyone to agree; it requires mutual respect, curiosity, and humility so we can prioritize understanding others over being understood by others. This is how we find common ground and seek a common good. Dialogue is crucial for community life; practicing it helps us model honesty, build trust, and decrease fear of difference and disagreement (no. 203). Robust dialogue gives us greater access to the truth, and "to learn how to unmask the various ways that the truth is manipulated, distorted and concealed in public and private discourse" (no. 208). It is not a form of relativism, where each person makes or decides their own truth and imposes it on others. Rather, it is the only way to make room for everyone and build consensus orbiting around "certain fundamental truths always to be upheld" (no. 211). These moral norms—like equality, mutual respect, and integrity—are the basis for the shared agreement and accountability that honors the "same inviolable dignity" of every human being (no. 213).

Dialogue resists the "throwaway culture" that can convince people that others are "insignificant, irrelevant, of no value to society" (no. 218). It can help us learn to see others as God sees them, as unique and precious, loved unconditionally, the cause of God's delight. This means that we must dialogue and build relationships with those pushed to the peripheries of our concern, the poor and powerless, those subjected to the violence of indifference, intolerance, and disrespect. The pope lifts up indigenous peoples as especially deserving of our dialogue and still awaiting integration as full and equal participants in society (no. 220). He invokes St. Paul's Letter to the Galatians (5:22), where kindness is described as a fruit of the Holy Spirit, expressed through "an attitude that is gentle, pleasant and supportive…[helping to] make other people's lives more bearable, especially by sharing the weight of their problems, needs, and fears" (no. 223). Kindness inspires us to reach out to others, to receive them as they are, and to work together for the conditions that allow people to be freely and fully alive. This is what holiness looks like, according to St. Irenaeus of Lyons: "The glory of God is the human person fully alive." To accomplish this vision, we have to break down walls built by deception, fear, suspicion, indifference, and hate. We have to build bridges of genuine interest and attention, mutual respect, and empathy. Only then can we celebrate diversity rather than tolerate it. Only then can neighbors and strangers become friends.

---

198. Approaching, speaking, listening, looking at, coming to know and understand one another, and to find common ground: all these things are summed up in the one word "dialogue." If we want to encounter and help one another, we have to dialogue. There is no need for me to stress the benefits of dialogue. I have only to think of what our world would be like without the patient dialogue of the many generous persons who keep families and communities together. Unlike disagreement and conflict, persistent and courageous dialogue does not make headlines, but quietly helps the world to live much better than we imagine.

SOCIAL DIALOGUE FOR A NEW CULTURE

199. Some people attempt to flee from reality, taking refuge in their own little world; others react to it with destructive violence. Yet "between selfish indifference and violent protest there is always another possible option: that of dialogue. Dialogue between generations; dialogue among our people, for we are that people; readiness to give and receive, while remaining open to the truth. A country flourishes when constructive dialogue occurs between its many rich cultural components: popular culture, university culture, youth culture, artistic culture, technological culture, economic culture, family culture and media culture."[196]

> "Some people attempt to flee from reality, taking refuge in their own little world; others react to it with destructive violence. Yet 'between selfish indifference and violent protest there is always another possible option: that of dialogue. Dialogue between generations; dialogue among our people, for we are that people; readiness to give and receive, while remaining open to the truth. A country flourishes when constructive dialogue occurs between its many rich cultural components: popular culture, university culture, youth culture, artistic culture, technological culture, economic culture, family culture and media culture'" (no. 199).

200. Dialogue is often confused with something quite different: the feverish exchange of opinions on social networks, frequently based on media information that is not always reliable. These exchanges are merely parallel monologues. They may

196. *Meeting with Brazilian Political, Economic and Cultural Leaders*, Rio de Janeiro, Brazil (27 July 2013): AAS 105 (2013), 683-684.

attract some attention by their sharp and aggressive tone. But monologues engage no one, and their content is frequently self-serving and contradictory.

201. Indeed, the media's noisy potpourri of facts and opinions is often an obstacle to dialogue, since it lets everyone cling stubbornly to his or her own ideas, interests and choices, with the excuse that everyone else is wrong. It becomes easier to discredit and insult opponents from the outset than to open a respectful dialogue aimed at achieving agreement on a deeper level. Worse, this kind of language, usually drawn from media coverage of political campaigns, has become so widespread as to be part of daily conversation. Discussion is often manipulated by powerful special interests that seek to tilt public opinion unfairly in their favour. This kind of manipulation can be exercised not only by governments, but also in economics, politics, communications, religion and in other spheres. Attempts can be made to justify or excuse it when it tends to serve one's own economic or ideological interests, but sooner or later it turns against those very interests.

202. Lack of dialogue means that in these individual sectors people are concerned not for the common good, but for the benefits of power or, at best, for ways to impose their own ideas. Round tables thus become mere negotiating sessions, in which individuals attempt to seize every possible advantage, rather than cooperating in the pursuit of the common good. The heroes of the future will be those who can break with this unhealthy mindset and determine respectfully to promote truthfulness, aside from personal interest. God willing, such heroes are quietly emerging, even now, in the midst of our society.

Building together

203. Authentic social dialogue involves the ability to respect the other's point of view and to admit that it may include legitimate convictions and concerns. Based on their identity and experience, others have a contribution to make, and it is desirable that they should articulate their positions for the sake of a more

fruitful public debate. When individuals or groups are consistent in their thinking, defend their values and convictions, and develop their arguments, this surely benefits society. Yet, this can only occur to the extent that there is genuine dialogue and openness to others. Indeed, "in a true spirit of dialogue, we grow in our ability to grasp the significance of what others say and do, even if we cannot accept it as our own conviction. In this way, it becomes possible to be frank and open about our beliefs, while continuing to discuss, to seek points of contact, and above all, to work and struggle together."[197] Public discussion, if it truly makes room for everyone and does not manipulate or conceal information, is a constant stimulus to a better grasp of the truth, or at least its more effective expression. It keeps different sectors from becoming complacent and self-centred in their outlook and their limited concerns. Let us not forget that "differences are creative; they create tension and in the resolution of tension lies humanity's progress."[198]

> "Authentic social dialogue involves the ability to respect the other's point of view and to admit that it may include legitimate convictions and concerns. Based on their identity and experience, others have a contribution to make, and it is desirable that they should articulate their positions for the sake of a more fruitful public debate. When individuals or groups are consistent in their thinking, defend their values and convictions, and develop their arguments, this surely benefits society. Yet, this can only occur to the extent that there is genuine dialogue and openness to others. Indeed, 'in a true spirit of dialogue, we grow in our ability to grasp the significance of what others say and do, even if we cannot accept it as our own conviction.

197. Apostolic Exhortation *Querida Amazonia* (2 February 2020), 108.
198. From the film *Pope Francis: A Man of His Word*, by Wim Wenders (2018).

In this way, it becomes possible to be frank and open about our beliefs, while continuing to discuss, to seek points of contact, and above all, to work and struggle together.' Public discussion, if it truly makes room for everyone and does not manipulate or conceal information, is a constant stimulus to a better grasp of the truth, or at least its more effective expression. It keeps different sectors from becoming complacent and self-centered in their outlook and their limited concerns. Let us not forget that 'differences are creative; they create tension and in the resolution of tension lies humanity's progress'" (no. 203).

204. There is a growing conviction that, together with specialized scientific advances, we are in need of greater interdisciplinary communication. Although reality is one, it can be approached from various angles and with different methodologies. There is a risk that a single scientific advance will be seen as the only possible lens for viewing a particular aspect of life, society and the world. Researchers who are expert in their own field, yet also familiar with the findings of other sciences and disciplines, are in a position to discern other aspects of the object of their study and thus to become open to a more comprehensive and integral knowledge of reality.

205. In today's globalized world, "the media can help us to feel closer to one another, creating a sense of the unity of the human family which in turn can inspire solidarity and serious efforts to ensure a more dignified life for all... The media can help us greatly in this, especially nowadays, when the networks of human communication have made unprecedented advances. The internet, in particular, offers immense possibilities for encounter and solidarity. This is something truly good, a gift from God."[199] We need constantly to ensure that present-day forms of

199. *Message for the 2014 World Communications Day* (24 January 2014): AAS 106 (2014), 113.

communication are in fact guiding us to generous encounter with others, to honest pursuit of the whole truth, to service, to closeness to the underprivileged and to the promotion of the common good. As the Bishops of Australia have pointed out, we cannot accept "a digital world designed to exploit our weaknesses and bring out the worst in people."[200]

THE BASIS OF CONSENSUS

206. The solution is not relativism. Under the guise of tolerance, relativism ultimately leaves the interpretation of moral values to those in power, to be defined as they see fit. "In the absence of objective truths or sound principles other than the satisfaction of our own desires and immediate needs… we should not think that political efforts or the force of law will be sufficient… When the culture itself is corrupt, and objective truth and universally valid principles are no longer upheld, then laws can only be seen as arbitrary impositions or obstacles to be avoided."[201]

207. Is it possible to be concerned for truth, to seek the truth that responds to life's deepest meaning? What is law without the conviction, born of age-old reflection and great wisdom, that each human being is sacred and inviolable? If society is to have a future, it must respect the truth of our human dignity and submit to that truth. Murder is not wrong simply because it is socially unacceptable and punished by law, but because of a deeper conviction. This is a non-negotiable truth attained by the use of reason and accepted in conscience. A society is noble and decent not least for its support of the pursuit of truth and its adherence to the most basic of truths.

208. We need to learn how to unmask the various ways that the truth is manipulated, distorted and concealed in public and

---

200. Australian Catholic Bishops' Conference, Commission for Social Justice, Mission and Service, *Making It Real: Genuine Human Encounter in Our Digital World* (November 2019).

201. Encyclical Letter *Laudato Si'* (24 May 2015), 123: AAS 107 (2015), 896.

private discourse. What we call "truth" is not only the reporting of facts and events, such as we find in the daily papers. It is primarily the search for the solid foundations sustaining our decisions and our laws. This calls for acknowledging that the human mind is capable of transcending immediate concerns and grasping certain truths that are unchanging, as true now as in the past. As it peers into human nature, reason discovers universal values derived from that same nature.

209. Otherwise, is it not conceivable that those fundamental human rights which we now consider unassailable will be denied by those in power, once they have gained the "consensus" of an apathetic or intimidated population? Nor would a mere consensus between different nations, itself equally open to manipulation, suffice to protect them. We have ample evidence of the great good of which we are capable, yet we also have to acknowledge our inherent destructiveness. Is not the indifference and the heartless individualism into which we have fallen also a result of our sloth in pursuing higher values, values that transcend our immediate needs? Relativism always brings the risk that some or other alleged truth will be imposed by the powerful or the clever. Yet, "when it is a matter of the moral norms prohibiting intrinsic evil, there are no privileges or exceptions for anyone. It makes no difference whether one is the master of the world or the 'poorest of the poor' on the face of the earth. Before the demands of morality we are all absolutely equal."[202]

210. What is now happening, and drawing us into a perverse and barren way of thinking, is the reduction of ethics and politics to physics. Good and evil no longer exist in themselves; there is only a calculus of benefits and burdens. As a result of the displacement of moral reasoning, the law is no longer seen as reflecting a fundamental notion of justice but as mirroring notions currently in vogue. Breakdown ensues: everything is "leveled down" by a superficial bartered consensus. In the end, the law of the strongest prevails.

202. Saint John Paul II, Encyclical Letter *Veritatis Splendor* (6 August 1993), 96: AAS 85 (1993), 1209.

Consensus and truth

211. In a pluralistic society, dialogue is the best way to realize what ought always to be affirmed and respected apart from any ephemeral consensus. Such dialogue needs to be enriched and illumined by clear thinking, rational arguments, a variety of perspectives and the contribution of different fields of knowledge and points of view. Nor can it exclude the conviction that it is possible to arrive at certain fundamental truths always to be upheld. Acknowledging the existence of certain enduring values, however demanding it may be to discern them, makes for a robust and solid social ethics. Once those fundamental values are acknowledged and adopted through dialogue and consensus, we realize that they rise above consensus; they transcend our concrete situations and remain non-negotiable. Our understanding of their meaning and scope can increase—and in that respect, consensus is a dynamic reality—but in themselves, they are held to be enduring by virtue of their inherent meaning.

212. If something always serves the good functioning of society, is it not because, lying beyond it, there is an enduring truth accessible to the intellect? Inherent in the nature of human beings and society there exist certain basic structures to support our development and survival. Certain requirements thus ensue, and these can be discovered through dialogue, even though, strictly speaking, they are not created by consensus. The fact that certain rules are indispensable for the very life of society is a sign that they are good in and of themselves. There is no need, then, to oppose the interests of society, consensus and the reality of objective truth. These three realities can be harmonized whenever, through dialogue, people are unafraid to get to the heart of an issue.

213. The dignity of others is to be respected in all circumstances, not because that dignity is something we have invented or imagined, but because human beings possess an intrinsic worth superior to that of material objects and contingent situations. This requires that they be treated differently. That every human being possesses an inalienable dignity is a truth that corresponds to human nature apart from all cultural change. For

this reason, human beings have the same inviolable dignity in every age of history and no one can consider himself or herself authorized by particular situations to deny this conviction or to act against it. The intellect can investigate the reality of things through reflection, experience and dialogue, and come to recognize in that reality, which transcends it, the basis of certain universal moral demands.

> "The dignity of others is to be respected in all circumstances, not because that dignity is something we have invented or imagined, but because human beings possess an intrinsic worth superior to that of material objects and contingent situations. This requires that they be treated differently. That every human being possesses an inalienable dignity is a truth that corresponds to human nature apart from all cultural change. For this reason, human beings have the same inviolable dignity in every age of history and no one can consider himself or herself authorized by particular situations to deny this conviction or to act against it. The intellect can investigate the reality of things through reflection, experience and dialogue, and come to recognize in that reality, which transcends it, the basis of certain universal moral demands" (no. 213).

214. To agnostics, this foundation could prove sufficient to confer a solid and stable universal validity on basic and non-negotiable ethical principles that could serve to prevent further catastrophes. As believers, we are convinced that human nature, as the source of ethical principles, was created by God, and that ultimately it is he who gives those principles their solid foundation.[203] This does not result in an ethical rigidity nor does it lead to

203. As Christians, we also believe that God grants us his grace to enable us to act as brothers and sisters.

the imposition of any one moral system, since fundamental and universally valid moral principles can be embodied in different practical rules. Thus, room for dialogue will always exist.

A NEW CULTURE

215. "Life, for all its confrontations, is the art of encounter."[204] I have frequently called for the growth of a culture of encounter capable of transcending our differences and divisions. This means working to create a many-faceted polyhedron whose different sides form a variegated unity, in which "the whole is greater than the part."[205] The image of a polyhedron can represent a society where differences coexist, complementing, enriching and reciprocally illuminating one another, even amid disagreements and reservations. Each of us can learn something from others. No one is useless and no one is expendable. This also means finding ways to include those on the peripheries of life. For they have another way of looking at things; they see aspects of reality that are invisible to the centres of power where weighty decisions are made.

Encounter that becomes culture

216. The word "culture" points to something deeply embedded within a people, its most cherished convictions and its way of life. A people's "culture" is more than an abstract idea. It has to do with their desires, their interests and ultimately the way they live their lives. To speak of a "culture of encounter" means that we, as a people, should be passionate about meeting others, seeking points of contact, building bridges, planning a project that includes everyone. This becomes an aspiration and a style of life. The subject of this culture is the people, not simply one part

---

204. Vinicius de moraes, *Samba da Benção*, from the recording *Um encontro no Au bon Gourmet*, Rio de Janeiro (2 August 1962).

205. Apostolic Exhortation *Evangelii Gaudium* (24 November 2013), 237: AAS 105 (2013), 1116.

of society that would pacify the rest with the help of professional and media resources.

> "To speak of a 'culture of encounter' means that we, as a people, should be passionate about meeting others, seeking points of contact, building bridges, planning a project that includes everyone. This becomes an aspiration and a style of life" (no. 216).

217. Social peace demands hard work, craftsmanship. It would be easier to keep freedoms and differences in check with cleverness and a few resources. But such a peace would be superficial and fragile, not the fruit of a culture of encounter that brings enduring stability. Integrating differences is a much more difficult and slow process, yet it is the guarantee of a genuine and lasting peace. That peace is not achieved by recourse only to those who are pure and untainted, since "even people who can be considered questionable on account of their errors have something to offer which must not be overlooked."[206] Nor does it come from ignoring social demands or quelling disturbances, since it is not "a consensus on paper or a transient peace for a contented minority."[207] What is important is to create *processes* of encounter, processes that build a people that can accept differences. Let us arm our children with the weapons of dialogue! Let us teach them to fight the good fight of the culture of encounter!

> "Social peace demands hard work, craftsmanship. It would be easier to keep freedoms and differences in check with cleverness and a few resources. But such a peace would be superficial and fragile, not the fruit of a culture of encounter that brings enduring stability. Integrating differences is a much more difficult and

206. Ibid., 236: AAS 105 (2013), 1115.
207. Ibid., 218: AAS 105 (2013), 1110.

slow process, yet it is the guarantee of a genuine and lasting peace.... What is important is to create *processes* of encounter, processes that build a people that can accept differences. Let us arm our children with the weapons of dialogue! Let us teach them to fight the good fight of the culture of encounter!" (no. 217).

The joy of acknowledging others

218. All this calls for the ability to recognize other people's right to be themselves and to be different. This recognition, as it becomes a culture, makes possible the creation of a social covenant. Without it, subtle ways can be found to make others insignificant, irrelevant, of no value to society. While rejecting certain visible forms of violence, another more insidious kind of violence can take root: the violence of those who despise people who are different, especially when their demands in any way compromise their own particular interests.

219. When one part of society exploits all that the world has to offer, acting as if the poor did not exist, there will eventually be consequences. Sooner or later, ignoring the existence and rights of others will erupt in some form of violence, often when least expected. Liberty, equality and fraternity can remain lofty ideals unless they apply to everyone. Encounter cannot take place only between the holders of economic, political or academic power. Genuine social encounter calls for a dialogue that engages the culture shared by the majority of the population. It often happens that good ideas are not accepted by the poorer sectors of society because they are presented in a cultural garb that is not their own and with which they cannot identify. A realistic and inclusive social covenant must also be a "cultural covenant," one that respects and acknowledges the different worldviews, cultures and lifestyles that coexist in society.

220. Indigenous peoples, for example, are not opposed to progress, yet theirs is a different notion of progress, often more humanistic than the modern culture of developed peoples.

Theirs is not a culture meant to benefit the powerful, those driven to create for themselves a kind of earthly paradise. Intolerance and lack of respect for indigenous popular cultures is a form of violence grounded in a cold and judgmental way of viewing them. No authentic, profound and enduring change is possible unless it starts from the different cultures, particularly those of the poor. A cultural covenant eschews a monolithic understanding of the identity of a particular place; it entails respect for diversity by offering opportunities for advancement and social integration to all.

221. Such a covenant also demands the realization that some things may have to be renounced for the common good. No one can possess the whole truth or satisfy his or her every desire, since that pretension would lead to nullifying others by denying their rights. A false notion of tolerance has to give way to a dialogic realism on the part of men and women who remain faithful to their own principles while recognizing that others also have the right to do likewise. This is the genuine acknowledgment of the other that is made possible by love alone. We have to stand in the place of others, if we are to discover what is genuine, or at least understandable, in their motivations and concerns.

RECOVERING KINDNESS

222. Consumerist individualism has led to great injustice. Other persons come to be viewed simply as obstacles to our own serene existence; we end up treating them as annoyances and we become increasingly aggressive. This is even more the case in times of crisis, catastrophe and hardship, when we are tempted to think in terms of the old saying, "every man for himself." Yet even then, we can choose to cultivate kindness. Those who do so become stars shining in the midst of darkness.

223. Saint Paul describes kindness as a fruit of the Holy Spirit (*Gal* 5:22). He uses the Greek word *chrestótes*, which describes an attitude that is gentle, pleasant and supportive, not rude or coarse. Individuals who possess this quality help make other people's lives

more bearable, especially by sharing the weight of their problems, needs and fears. This way of treating others can take different forms: an act of kindness, a concern not to offend by word or deed, a readiness to alleviate their burdens. It involves "speaking words of comfort, strength, consolation and encouragement" and not "words that demean, sadden, anger or show scorn."[208]

224. Kindness frees us from the cruelty that at times infects human relationships, from the anxiety that prevents us from thinking of others, from the frantic flurry of activity that forgets that others also have a right to be happy. Often nowadays we find neither the time nor the energy to stop and be kind to others, to say "excuse me," "pardon me," "thank you." Yet every now and then, miraculously, a kind person appears and is willing to set everything else aside in order to show interest, to give the gift of a smile, to speak a word of encouragement, to listen amid general indifference. If we make a daily effort to do exactly this, we can create a healthy social atmosphere in which misunderstandings can be overcome and conflict forestalled. Kindness ought to be cultivated; it is no superficial bourgeois virtue. Precisely because it entails esteem and respect for others, once kindness becomes a culture within society it transforms lifestyles, relationships and the ways ideas are discussed and compared. Kindness facilitates the quest for consensus; it opens new paths where hostility and conflict would burn all bridges.

QUESTIONS FOR REFLECTION AND DISCUSSION

1. Pope Francis describes dialogue through these actions: "approaching, speaking, listening, looking at, coming to know and understand one another, and to find common ground" (no. 198). What obstacles do we have to

208. Apostolic Exhortation *Amoris Laetitia* (19 March 2016), 100: AAS 108 (2016), 351.

overcome in order to make a habit of these acts? How can you try to practice greater courage, compassion, and patience in your willingness to make others feel heard? What do you need to feel heard by others—and how can you make that known?

2. Paragraph 203 articulates a robust defense of dialogue, especially one that "truly makes room for everyone." Who are the people in your life who may feel unseen and unheard? Who are the people in your community who get sidelined from participating in dialogue? How can you use your position and relationships to make sure more people get a "seat at the table"? Or, if that's not possible, what alternatives exist in order to create settings where more people feel welcome?
3. We know that so much interpersonal communication is expressed nonverbally (through facial expressions, gestures, and body posture, for example), and a lot of that is lost through digital interactions. How does this chapter invite you to reconsider how you share with and receive others online? Pope Francis cites the bishops of Australia in stating, "We cannot accept 'a digital world designed to exploit our weaknesses and bring out the worst in people'" (no. 205). How can you be part of a digital transformation in saying—and receiving—the truth with love?
4. Pope Francis reminds us that while every person bears equal human dignity, this should not minimize our differences. In fact, our differences mean that people should not always be treated identically. The Golden Rule—treat others as you would want to be treated—might be improved by the Platinum Rule—treat others as they want to be treated—since we don't always know what others want or need. If you were to practice the Platinum Rule in your life, what difference would it make for you? For others?

5. One of Dorothy Day's favorite lines was the "duty of delight," to bask in the goodness of others. How might this change our perspective of dialogue from a burdensome obligation to an enlivening opportunity to better understand the world from the experience of someone who is not me? In the face of anxiety and the "frantic flurry of activity" that can make us insecure or forgetful about acknowledging, accepting, and affirming others, how can we embrace the "duty of delight" as a habit of kindness and respect, showing others they are worthy of our time, our full presence, and our willingness to be conversation partners (no. 224)?

FOR FURTHER READING

Doak, Mary. *Divine Harmony: Seeking Community in a Broken World*. Mahwah, NJ: Paulist Press, 2016.

John of Taizé, Brother. *Friends in Christ: Paths to a New Understanding of Church*. Maryknoll, NY: Orbis Books, 2012.

Regan, Jane E. *Where Two or Three Are Gathered: Transforming the Parish through Communities of Practice*. Mahwah, NJ: Paulist Press, 2016.

Stiltner, Brian. *Toward Thriving Communities: Virtue Ethics as Social Ethics*. Winona, MN: Anselm Academic, 2016.

Wadell, Paul J. *Becoming Friends: Worship, Justice, and the Practice of Christian Friendship*. Grand Rapids, MI: Brazos Press, 2002.

Chapter Seven

PATHS OF RENEWED ENCOUNTER

SYNOPSIS

This chapter presents solidarity as a shared project advanced by practicing truth, mercy, forgiveness, justice, and peace. It focuses especially on what is needed to break the cycle of violence "which seems inescapable" (no. 227). Pope Francis does not pose an abstract theory of peace as tranquility or the absence of conflict; *Fratelli Tutti* draws on the experience of the church all over the globe, weaving in insights from Congo to Colombia, from Albania to South Korea, from Jerusalem to Hiroshima. There is no path to peace without solidarity; solidarity is impossible without peace.

This chapter repeats the need to celebrate—not merely tolerate—diversity. Pope Francis explains, "The path to peace does not mean making society blandly uniform, but getting people to work together, side-by-side, in pursuing goals that benefit everyone. A wide variety of practical proposals and diverse experiences can help achieve shared objectives and serve the common good" (no. 228). The way to do this, the pope suggests, is to see our society like a family: not immune from disputes, but always seeking resolution after conflict. While this might be a flawed analogy (not all families experience reconciliation and families are too often home to asymmetrical if not abusive exercises of power), his intention is to harness the closeness, affinity, and shared commitment inspired by many people's experience of family life and turn this outward, in service to a society oriented toward human dignity and the common good. Pope Francis hopes that this will "help us flee from the temptation for revenge and the satisfaction of short-term partisan interests" (no. 232).

Returning to a familiar theme, Pope Francis places the poor and vulnerable at the center of our peace-making efforts. This is necessary "to recognize, protect and concretely restore the dignity, so often overlooked or ignored, of our brothers and sisters, so that they can see themselves as the principal protagonists of the destiny of their nation" (no. 233). It also implies sharing life with the marginalized, since "only the closeness that makes us friends can enable us to appreciate deeply the values of the poor today, their legitimate desires, and their own manner of living the faith. The option for the poor should lead us to friendship with the poor" (no. 234). These firsthand encounters remind us that "inequality and lack of integral human development make peace impossible" by putting us in touch with deprivation and desperation (no. 235). When we embrace solidarity as a social friendship, the problems our friends face become our own problems, as well.

The next section of this chapter focuses on forgiveness and reconciliation as central to Christian faith and discipleship. Pope Francis turns our attention to the example of the earliest Christian communities, which endured persecution and aimed to respond with gentleness, even in the face of legitimate conflict (nos. 239–43). *Fratelli Tutti* makes clear that Christians should not adopt a posture of apathy, intolerance, or fatalism; nor should they embrace hatred or seek vengeance, since "nothing is gained this way and, in the end, everything is lost" (no. 242). Forgiveness is possible when we seek to uncover the truth, enhance our understanding, and share the commitment to deliver what each person deserves in order to restore what has been broken. It must be a personal choice, not imposed like a "blanket act" on any individual or group. Pope Francis also clarifies that if our goals are forgiveness and reconciliation, "forgetting is never the answer" (no. 246). He points to the Holocaust and atomic bombs as two of the darkest moments in human history, which we must share with future generations so we avoid repeating these barbaric acts of persecution and violence—even though, he acknowledges, people continue to suffer at the hands of slave trade and genocide. Pope Francis resolves, "They need to be remembered, always and ever anew. We must never grow accustomed or inured to them" (no. 248).*

The final section of this chapter focuses on the injustice of war and the need to abolish the death penalty. Pope Francis attests, "War is not a ghost from the past but a constant threat" (no. 256). War violates human dignity, destroys communities, and ravages the environment. He contends, "Every war leaves our world worse than it was before" (no. 261) and accuses proponents of the just war tradition as too easily justifying violence—even invoking the right to defense to excuse preemptive attacks. The pope explains (and perhaps

* Pope Francis's emphasis on remembering the Holocaust is especially needed in light of the rise of anti-Semitic speech and hate crimes in the United States. According to a study published just before *Fratelli Tutti*, nearly two-thirds of American young adults don't know that 6 million Jews were killed during the Holocaust, and almost a quarter said the Holocaust was a myth, exaggerated, or unsure of what to believe about it. See, e.g., Harriet Sherwood, "Nearly Two-Thirds of US Young Adults Unaware 6m Jews Killed in the Holocaust," *The Guardian*, September 16, 2020, https://www.theguardian.com/world/2020/sep/16/holocaust-us-adults-study.

points to a future encyclical) that the question is "whether the development of nuclear, chemical and biological weapons, and the enormous and growing possibilities offered by new technologies, have granted war an uncontrollable destructive power over great numbers of innocent civilians." He concludes with clear and compelling words, "We can no longer think of war as a solution, because its risks will probably always be greater than its supposed benefits. In view of this, it is very difficult nowadays to invoke the rational criteria elaborated in earlier centuries to speak of the possibility of a 'just war.' Never again war!" (no. 258).† Pope Francis also condemns militarization and arms sales, proposing that the money spent on weapons and the military should be used to "establish a global fund that can finally put an end to hunger and favour development in the most impoverished countries, so that their citizens will not resort to violent or illusory solutions, or have to leave their countries in order to seek a more dignified life" (no. 262). He concludes this portion of the encyclical dedicating several paragraphs imploring,

> All Christians and people of good will are today called to work not only for the abolition of the death penalty, legal or illegal, in all its forms, but also to work for the improvement of prison conditions, out of respect for the human dignity of persons deprived of their freedom. I would link this to life imprisonment… A life sentence is a secret death penalty. (no. 268)

† Unfortunately, however, this section does not include an overview of the possibilities—present and future—for resolving and preventing conflict through a commitment to nonviolence. For more on this subject, see Eli S. McCarthy, ed., *A Just Peace Ethic Primer: Building Sustainable Peace and Breaking Cycles of Violence* (Washington, DC: Georgetown University Press, 2020).

Authentic forgiveness and reconciliation require such a different worldview, beliefs, and practices than what the criminal justice systems and defense budget have in place. With this chapter, the pope urges us to heed the words of the prophetic tradition where the faithful "beat their swords into plowshares" (Isa 2:4) since we will have to answer for the lives of our siblings in God's single family (Gen 9:5–6).

---

225. In many parts of the world, there is a need for paths of peace to heal open wounds. There is also a need for peacemakers, men and women prepared to work boldly and creatively to initiate processes of healing and renewed encounter.

STARTING ANEW FROM THE TRUTH

226. Renewed encounter does not mean returning to a time prior to conflicts. All of us change over time. Pain and conflict transform us. We no longer have use for empty diplomacy, dissimulation, double-speak, hidden agendas and good manners that mask reality. Those who were fierce enemies have to speak from the stark and clear truth. They have to learn how to cultivate a penitential memory, one that can accept the past in order not to cloud the future with their own regrets, problems and plans. Only by basing themselves on the historical truth of events will they be able to make a broad and persevering effort to understand one another and to strive for a new synthesis for the good of all. Every "peace process requires enduring commitment. It is a patient effort to seek truth and justice, to honour the memory of victims and to open the way, step by step, to a shared hope stronger than the desire for vengeance."[209] As the Bishops of the Congo have said with regard to one recurring conflict: "Peace agreements on paper will not be enough. We will

209. *Message for the 2020 World Day of Peace* (8 December 2019), 2: *L'Osservatore Romano*, 13 December 2019, p. 8.

have to go further, by respecting the demands of truth regarding the origins of this recurring crisis. The people have the right to know what happened."[210]

> "Renewed encounter does not mean returning to a time prior to conflicts. All of us change over time. Pain and conflict transform us. We no longer have use for empty diplomacy, dissimulation, double-speak, hidden agendas and good manners that mask reality. Those who were fierce enemies have to speak from the stark and clear truth. They have to learn how to cultivate a penitential memory, one that can accept the past in order not to cloud the future with their own regrets, problems and plans. Only by basing themselves on the historical truth of events will they be able to make a broad and persevering effort to understand one another and to strive for a new synthesis for the good of all. Every 'peace process requires enduring commitment. It is a patient effort to seek truth and justice, to honor the memory of victims and to open the way, step by step, to a shared hope stronger than the desire for vengeance'" (no. 226).

227. "Truth, in fact, is an inseparable companion of justice and mercy. All three together are essential to building peace; each, moreover, prevents the other from being altered... Truth should not lead to revenge, but rather to reconciliation and forgiveness. Truth means telling families torn apart by pain what happened to their missing relatives. Truth means confessing what happened to minors recruited by cruel and violent people. Truth means recognizing the pain of women who are victims of violence and abuse... Every act of violence committed against a

210. Episcopal Conference of the Congo, *Message au Peuple de Dieu et aux femmes et aux hommes de bonne volonté* (9 May 2018).

human being is a wound in humanity's flesh; every violent death diminishes us as people... Violence leads to more violence, hatred to more hatred, death to more death. We must break this cycle which seems inescapable."[211]

THE ART AND ARCHITECTURE OF PEACE

228. The path to peace does not mean making society blandly uniform, but getting people to work together, side-by-side, in pursuing goals that benefit everyone. A wide variety of practical proposals and diverse experiences can help achieve shared objectives and serve the common good. The problems that a society is experiencing need to be clearly identified, so that the existence of different ways of understanding and resolving them can be appreciated. The path to social unity always entails acknowledging the possibility that others have, at least in part, a legitimate point of view, something worthwhile to contribute, even if they were in error or acted badly. "We should never confine others to what they may have said or done, but value them for the promise that they embody,"[212] a promise that always brings with it a spark of new hope.

229. The Bishops of South Africa have pointed out that true reconciliation is achieved proactively, "by forming a new society, a society based on service to others, rather than the desire to dominate; a society based on sharing what one has with others, rather than the selfish scramble by each for as much wealth as possible; a society in which the value of being together as human beings is ultimately more important than any lesser group, whether it be family, nation, race or culture."[213] As the Bishops of

211. *Address at the National Reconciliation Encounter*, Villavicencio, Colombia (8 September 2017): AAS 109 (2017), 1063–1064, 1066.

212. *Message for the 2020 World Day of Peace* (8 December 2019), 3: *L'Osservatore Romano*, 13 December 2019, p. 8.

213. Southern African Catholic Bishops' Conference, *Pastoral Letter on Christian Hope in the Current Crisis* (May 1986).

South Korea have pointed out, true peace "can be achieved only when we strive for justice through dialogue, pursuing reconciliation and mutual development."[214]

230. Working to overcome our divisions without losing our identity as individuals presumes that a basic sense of belonging is present in everyone. Indeed, "society benefits when each person and social group feels truly at home. In a family, parents, grandparents and children all feel at home; no one is excluded. If someone has a problem, even a serious one, even if he brought it upon himself, the rest of the family comes to his assistance; they support him. His problems are theirs... In families, everyone contributes to the common purpose; everyone works for the common good, not denying each person's individuality but encouraging and supporting it. They may quarrel, but there is something that does not change: the family bond. Family disputes are always resolved afterwards. The joys and sorrows of each of its members are felt by all. That is what it means to be a family! If only we could view our political opponents or neighbours in the same way that we view our children or our spouse, mother or father! How good would this be! Do we love our society or is it still something remote, something anonymous that does not involve us, something to which we are not committed?"[215]

231. Negotiation often becomes necessary for shaping concrete paths to peace. Yet the processes of change that lead to lasting peace are crafted above all by peoples; each individual can act as an effective leaven by the way he or she lives each day. Great changes are not produced behind desks or in offices. This means that "everyone has a fundamental role to play in a single great creative project: to write a new page of history, a page full of hope, peace and reconciliation."[216] There is an "architecture" of peace, to which different institutions of society contribute,

---

214. Catholic Bishops' Conference of Korea, *Appeal of the Catholic Church in Korea for Peace on the Korean Peninsula* (15 August 2017).

215. Meeting with Political, Economic and Civic Leaders, Quito, Ecuador (7 July 2015): *L'Osservatore Romano*, 9 July 2015, p. 9.

216. *Interreligious Meeting with Youth*, Maputo, Mozambique (5 September 2019): *L'Osservatore Romano*, 6 September 2019, p. 7.

each according to its own area of expertise, but there is also an "art" of peace that involves us all. From the various peace processes that have taken place in different parts of the world, "we have learned that these ways of making peace, of placing reason above revenge, of the delicate harmony between politics and law, cannot ignore the involvement of ordinary people. Peace is not achieved by normative frameworks and institutional arrangements between well-meaning political or economic groups... It is always helpful to incorporate into our peace processes the experience of those sectors that have often been overlooked, so that communities themselves can influence the development of a collective memory."[217]

232. There is no end to the building of a country's social peace; rather, it is "an open-ended endeavour, a never-ending task that demands the commitment of everyone and challenges us to work tirelessly to build the unity of the nation. Despite obstacles, differences and varying perspectives on the way to achieve peaceful coexistence, this task summons us to persevere in the struggle to promote a 'culture of encounter.' This requires us to place at the centre of all political, social and economic activity the human person, who enjoys the highest dignity, and respect for the common good. May this determination help us flee from the temptation for revenge and the satisfaction of short-term partisan interests."[218] Violent public demonstrations, on one side or the other, do not help in finding solutions. Mainly because, as the Bishops of Colombia have rightly noted, the "origins and objectives of civil demonstrations are not always clear; certain forms of political manipulation are present and in some cases they have been exploited for partisan interests."[219]

---

217. *Homily*, Cartagena de Indias, Colombia (10 September 2017): AAS 109 (2017), 1086.

218. *Meeting with Authorities, the Diplomatic Corps and Representatives of Civil Society*, Bogotá, Colombia (7 September 2017): AAS 109 (2017), 1029.

219. Bishops' Conference of Colombia, *Por el bien de Colombia: diálogo, reconciliación y desarrollo integral* (26 November 2019), 4.

Beginning with the least

233. Building social friendship does not only call for rapprochement between groups who took different sides at some troubled period of history, but also for a renewed encounter with the most impoverished and vulnerable sectors of society. For peace "is not merely absence of war but a tireless commitment—especially on the part of those of us charged with greater responsibility—to recognize, protect and concretely restore the dignity, so often overlooked or ignored, of our brothers and sisters, so that they can see themselves as the principal protagonists of the destiny of their nation."[220]

234. Often, the more vulnerable members of society are the victims of unfair generalizations. If at times the poor and the dispossessed react with attitudes that appear antisocial, we should realize that in many cases those reactions are born of a history of scorn and social exclusion. The Latin American Bishops have observed that "only the closeness that makes us friends can enable us to appreciate deeply the values of the poor today, their legitimate desires, and their own manner of living the faith. The option for the poor should lead us to friendship with the poor."[221]

235. Those who work for tranquil social coexistence should never forget that inequality and lack of integral human development make peace impossible. Indeed, "without equal opportunities, different forms of aggression and conflict will find a fertile terrain for growth and eventually explode. When a society—whether local, national or global—is willing to leave a part of itself on the fringes, no political programmes or resources spent on law enforcement or surveillance systems can indefinitely guarantee tranquility."[222] If we have to begin anew, it must always be from the least of our brothers and sisters.

---

220. *Meeting with the Authorities, Civil Society and the Diplomatic Corps*, Maputo, Mozambique (5 September 2019): *L'Osservatore Romano*, 6 September 2019, p. 6.

221. Fifth General Conference of the Latin American and Caribbean Bishops, *Aparecida Document* (29 June 2007), 398.

222. Apostolic Exhortation *Evangelii Gaudium* (24 November 2013), 59: AAS 105 (2013), 1044.

THE VALUE AND MEANING OF FORGIVENESS

236. There are those who prefer not to talk of reconciliation, for they think that conflict, violence and breakdown are part of the normal functioning of a society. In any human group there are always going to be more or less subtle power struggles between different parties. Others think that promoting forgiveness means yielding ground and influence to others. For this reason, they feel it is better to keep things as they are, maintaining a balance of power between differing groups. Still others believe that reconciliation is a sign of weakness; incapable of truly serious dialogue, they choose to avoid problems by ignoring injustices. Unable to deal with problems, they opt for an apparent peace.

Inevitable conflict

237. Forgiveness and reconciliation are central themes in Christianity and, in various ways, in other religions. Yet there is a risk that an inadequate understanding and presentation of these profound convictions can lead to fatalism, apathy and injustice, or even intolerance and violence.

238. Jesus never promoted violence or intolerance. He openly condemned the use of force to gain power over others: "You know that the rulers of the Gentiles lord it over them, and their great ones are tyrants over them. It will not be so among you" (*Mt* 20:25–26). Instead, the Gospel tells us to forgive "seventy times seven" (*Mt* 18:22) and offers the example of the unmerciful servant who was himself forgiven, yet unable to forgive others in turn (cf. *Mt* 18:23–35).

239. Reading other texts of the New Testament, we can see how the early Christian communities, living in a pagan world marked by widespread corruption and aberrations, sought to show unfailing patience, tolerance and understanding. Some texts are very clear in this regard: we are told to admonish our opponents "with gentleness" (*2 Tim* 2:25) and encouraged "to

speak evil of no one, to avoid quarreling, to be gentle, and to show every courtesy to everyone. For we ourselves were once foolish" (*Tit* 3:2–3). The Acts of the Apostles notes that the disciples, albeit persecuted by some of the authorities, "had favour with all the people" (2:47; cf. 4:21.33; 5:13).

240. Yet when we reflect upon forgiveness, peace and social harmony, we also encounter the jarring saying of Christ: "Do not think that I have come to bring peace to the earth; I have not come to bring peace, but a sword. For I have come to set a man against his father, and a daughter against her mother, and a daughter-in-law against her mother-in-law; and a man's foes will be members of his own household" (*Mt* 10:34–36). These words need to be understood in the context of the chapter in which they are found, where it is clear that Jesus is speaking of fidelity to our decision to follow him; we are not to be ashamed of that decision, even if it entails hardships of various sorts, and even our loved ones refuse to accept it. Christ's words do not encourage us to seek conflict, but simply to endure it when it inevitably comes, lest deference to others, for the sake of supposed peace in our families or society, should detract from our own fidelity. Saint John Paul II observed that the Church "does not intend to condemn every possible form of social conflict. The Church is well aware that in the course of history conflicts of interest between different social groups inevitably arise, and that in the face of such conflicts Christians must often take a position, honestly and decisively."[223]

Legitimate conflict and forgiveness

241. Nor does this mean calling for forgiveness when it involves renouncing our own rights, confronting corrupt officials, criminals or those who would debase our dignity. We are called to love everyone, without exception; at the same time, loving an oppressor does not mean allowing him to keep oppressing us, or letting him think that what he does is acceptable. On the contrary, true love for an oppressor means seeking ways to make him

223. Encyclical Letter *Centesimus Annus* (1 May 1991), 14: AAS 83 (1991), 810.

cease his oppression; it means stripping him of a power that he does not know how to use, and that diminishes his own humanity and that of others. Forgiveness does not entail allowing oppressors to keep trampling on their own dignity and that of others, or letting criminals continue their wrongdoing. Those who suffer injustice have to defend strenuously their own rights and those of their family, precisely because they must preserve the dignity they have received as a loving gift from God. If a criminal has harmed me or a loved one, no one can forbid me from demanding justice and ensuring that this person—or anyone else—will not harm me, or others, again. This is entirely just; forgiveness does not forbid it but actually demands it.

> "Nor does this mean calling for forgiveness when it involves renouncing our own rights, confronting corrupt officials, criminals or those who would debase our dignity. We are called to love everyone, without exception; at the same time, loving an oppressor does not mean allowing him to keep oppressing us, or letting him think that what he does is acceptable. On the contrary, true love for an oppressor means seeking ways to make him cease his oppression; it means stripping him of a power that he does not know how to use, and that diminishes his own humanity and that of others. Forgiveness does not entail allowing oppressors to keep trampling on their own dignity and that of others, or letting criminals continue their wrongdoing. Those who suffer injustice have to defend strenuously their own rights and those of their family, precisely because they must preserve the dignity they have received as a loving gift from God. If a criminal has harmed me or a loved one, no one can forbid me from demanding justice and ensuring that this person—or anyone else—will not harm me, or others, again. This is entirely just;

forgiveness does not forbid it but actually demands it" (no. 241).

242. The important thing is not to fuel anger, which is unhealthy for our own soul and the soul of our people, or to become obsessed with taking revenge and destroying the other. No one achieves inner peace or returns to a normal life in that way. The truth is that "no family, no group of neighbours, no ethnic group, much less a nation, has a future if the force that unites them, brings them together and resolves their differences is vengeance and hatred. We cannot come to terms and unite for the sake of revenge, or treating others with the same violence with which they treated us, or plotting opportunities for retaliation under apparently legal auspices."[224] Nothing is gained this way and, in the end, everything is lost.

243. To be sure, "it is no easy task to overcome the bitter legacy of injustices, hostility and mistrust left by conflict. It can only be done by overcoming evil with good (cf. *Rom* 12:21) and by cultivating those virtues which foster reconciliation, solidarity and peace."[225] In this way, "persons who nourish goodness in their heart find that such goodness leads to a peaceful conscience and to profound joy, even in the midst of difficulties and misunderstandings. Even when affronted, goodness is never weak but rather, shows its strength by refusing to take revenge."[226] Each of us should realize that "even the harsh judgment I hold in my heart against my brother or my sister, the open wound that was never cured, the offense that was never forgiven, the rancour that is only going to hurt me, are all instances of a struggle that I

---

224. *Homily at Mass for the Progress of Peoples*, Maputo, Mozambique (6 September 2019): *L'Osservatore Romano*, 7 September 2019, p. 8.

225. *Arrival Ceremony*, Colombo, Sri Lanka (13 January2015): *L'Osservatore Romano*, 14 January 2015, p. 7.

226. *Meeting with the Children of the "Bethany Centre" and Representatives of other Charitable Centres of Albania*, Tirana, Albania (21 September 2014): *Insegnamenti* II, 2 (2014), 288.

carry within me, a little flame deep in my heart that needs to be extinguished before it turns into a great blaze."[227]

The best way to move on

244. When conflicts are not resolved but kept hidden or buried in the past, silence can lead to complicity in grave misdeeds and sins. Authentic reconciliation does not flee from conflict, but is achieved *in* conflict, resolving it through dialogue and open, honest and patient negotiation. Conflict between different groups "if it abstains from enmities and mutual hatred, gradually changes into an honest discussion of differences founded on a desire for justice."[228]

245. On numerous occasions, I have spoken of "a principle indispensable to the building of friendship in society: namely, that unity is greater than conflict… This is not to opt for a kind of syncretism, or for the absorption of one into the other, but rather for a resolution which takes place on a higher plane and preserves what is valid and useful on both sides."[229] All of us know that "when we, as individuals and communities, learn to look beyond ourselves and our particular interests, then understanding and mutual commitment bear fruit… in a setting where conflicts, tensions and even groups once considered inimical can attain a multifaceted unity that gives rise to new life."[230]

MEMORY

246. Of those who have endured much unjust and cruel suffering, a sort of "social forgiveness" must not be demanded.

227. *Video Message to the TED Conference in Vancouver* (26 April 2017): *L'Osservatore Romano*, 27 April 2017, p. 7.

228. Pius XI, Encyclical Letter *Quadragesimo Anno* (15 May 1931): AAS 23 (1931), 213.

229. Apostolic Exhortation *Evangelii Gaudium* (24 November 2013), 228: AAS 105 (2013), 1113.

230. *Meeting with the Civil Authorities, Civil Society and the Diplomatic Corps*, Riga, Latvia (24 September 2018): *L'Osservatore Romano*, 24–25 September 2018, p. 7.

Reconciliation is a personal act, and no one can impose it upon an entire society, however great the need to foster it. In a strictly personal way, someone, by a free and generous decision, can choose not to demand punishment (cf. *Mt* 5:44–46), even if it is quite legitimately demanded by society and its justice system. However, it is not possible to proclaim a "blanket reconciliation" in an effort to bind wounds by decree or to cover injustices in a cloak of oblivion. Who can claim the right to forgive in the name of others? It is moving to see forgiveness shown by those who are able to leave behind the harm they suffered, but it is also humanly understandable in the case of those who cannot. In any case, forgetting is never the answer.

247. The *Shoah* must not be forgotten. It is "the enduring symbol of the depths to which human evil can sink when, spurred by false ideologies, it fails to recognize the fundamental dignity of each person, which merits unconditional respect regardless of ethnic origin or religious belief."[231] As I think of it, I cannot help but repeat this prayer: "Lord, remember us in your mercy. Grant us the grace to be ashamed of what we men have done, to be ashamed of this massive idolatry, of having despised and destroyed our own flesh which you formed from the earth, to which you gave life with your own breath of life. Never again, Lord, never again!"[232]

248. Nor must we forget the atomic bombs dropped on Hiroshima and Nagasaki. Once again, "I pay homage to all the victims, and I bow before the strength and dignity of those who, having survived those first moments, for years afterward bore in the flesh immense suffering, and in their spirit seeds of death that drained their vital energy… We cannot allow present and future generations to lose the memory of what happened. It is a memory that ensures and encourages the building of a more fair and fraternal future."[233] Neither must we forget the persecutions, the

---

231. *Arrival Ceremony*, Tel Aviv, Israel (25 May 2014): *Insegnamenti* II, 1 (2014), 604.

232. *Visit to the Yad Vashem Memorial*, Jerusalem (26 May 2014): AAS 106 (2014), 228.

233. *Address at the Peace Memorial*, Hiroshima, Japan (24 November 2019): *L'Osservatore Romano*, 25–26 November 2019, p. 8.

slave trade and the ethnic killings that continue in various countries, as well as the many other historical events that make us ashamed of our humanity. They need to be remembered, always and ever anew. We must never grow accustomed or inured to them.

249. Nowadays, it is easy to be tempted to turn the page, to say that all these things happened long ago and we should look to the future. For God's sake, no! We can never move forward without remembering the past; we do not progress without an honest and unclouded memory. We need to "keep alive the flame of collective conscience, bearing witness to succeeding generations to the horror of what happened," because that witness "awakens and preserves the memory of the victims, so that the conscience of humanity may rise up in the face of every desire for dominance and destruction."[234] The victims themselves—individuals, social groups or nations—need to do so, lest they succumb to the mindset that leads to justifying reprisals and every kind of violence in the name of the great evil endured. For this reason, I think not only of the need to remember the atrocities, but also all those who, amid such great inhumanity and corruption, retained their dignity and, with gestures small or large, chose the part of solidarity, forgiveness and fraternity. To remember goodness is also a healthy thing.

Forgiving but not forgetting

250. Forgiving does not mean forgetting. Or better, in the face of a reality that can in no way be denied, relativized or concealed, forgiveness is still possible. In the face of an action that can never be tolerated, justified or excused, we can still forgive. In the face of something that cannot be forgotten for any reason, we can still forgive. Free and heartfelt forgiveness is something noble, a reflection of God's own infinite ability to forgive. If forgiveness is

234. *Message for the 2020 World Day of Peace* (8 December 2019), 2: *L'Osservatore Romano*, 13 December 2019, p. 8.

gratuitous, then it can be shown even to someone who resists repentance and is unable to beg pardon.

251. Those who truly forgive do not forget. Instead, they choose not to yield to the same destructive force that caused them so much suffering. They break the vicious circle; they halt the advance of the forces of destruction. They choose not to spread in society the spirit of revenge that will sooner or later return to take its toll. Revenge never truly satisfies victims. Some crimes are so horrendous and cruel that the punishment of those who perpetrated them does not serve to repair the harm done. Even killing the criminal would not be enough, nor could any form of torture prove commensurate with the sufferings inflicted on the victim. Revenge resolves nothing.

252. This does not mean impunity. Justice is properly sought solely out of love of justice itself, out of respect for the victims, as a means of preventing new crimes and protecting the common good, not as an alleged outlet for personal anger. Forgiveness is precisely what enables us to pursue justice without falling into a spiral of revenge or the injustice of forgetting.

253. When injustices have occurred on both sides, it is important to take into clear account whether they were equally grave or in any way comparable. Violence perpetrated by the state, using its structures and power, is not on the same level as that perpetrated by particular groups. In any event, one cannot claim that the unjust sufferings of one side alone should be commemorated. The Bishops of Croatia have stated that, "we owe equal respect to every innocent victim. There can be no racial, national, confessional or partisan differences."[235]

254. I ask God "to prepare our hearts to encounter our brothers and sisters, so that we may overcome our differences rooted in political thinking, language, culture and religion. Let us ask him to anoint our whole being with the balm of his mercy, which heals the injuries caused by mistakes, misunderstandings and disputes. And let us ask him for the grace to send us forth, in

235. Croatian Bishops' Conference, *Letter on the Fiftieth Anniversary of the End of the Second World War* (1 May 1995).

humility and meekness, along the demanding but enriching path of seeking peace."[236]

WAR AND THE DEATH PENALTY

255. There are two extreme situations that may come to be seen as solutions in especially dramatic circumstances, without realizing that they are false answers that do not resolve the problems they are meant to solve and ultimately do no more than introduce new elements of destruction in the fabric of national and global society. These are war and the death penalty.

The injustice of war

256. "Deceit is in the mind of those who plan evil, but those who counsel peace have joy" (*Prov* 12:20). Yet there are those who seek solutions in war, frequently fueled by a breakdown in relations, hegemonic ambitions, abuses of power, fear of others and a tendency to see diversity as an obstacle.[237] War is not a ghost from the past but a constant threat. Our world is encountering growing difficulties on the slow path to peace upon which it had embarked and which had already begun to bear good fruit.

257. Since conditions that favour the outbreak of wars are once again increasing, I can only reiterate that "war is the negation of all rights and a dramatic assault on the environment. If we want true integral human development for all, we must work tirelessly to avoid war between nations and peoples. To this end, there is a need to ensure the uncontested rule of law and tireless recourse to negotiation, mediation and arbitration, as proposed by the *Charter of the United Nations*, which constitutes truly a fundamental juridical norm."[238] The seventy-five years since the

236. *Homily*, Amman, Jordan (24 May 2014): *Insegnamenti* II, 1 (2014), 593.

237. Cf. *Message for the 2020 World Day of Peace* (8 December 2019), 1: *L'Osservatore Romano*, 13 December 2019, p. 8.

238. *Address to the Members of the General Assembly of the United Nations*, New

establishment of the United Nations and the experience of the first twenty years of this millennium have shown that the full application of international norms proves truly effective, and that failure to comply with them is detrimental. The *Charter of the United Nations*, when observed and applied with transparency and sincerity, is an obligatory reference point of justice and a channel of peace. Here there can be no room for disguising false intentions or placing the partisan interests of one country or group above the global common good. If rules are considered simply as means to be used whenever it proves advantageous, and to be ignored when it is not, uncontrollable forces are unleashed that cause grave harm to societies, to the poor and vulnerable, to fraternal relations, to the environment and to cultural treasures, with irretrievable losses for the global community.

258. War can easily be chosen by invoking all sorts of allegedly humanitarian, defensive or precautionary excuses, and even resorting to the manipulation of information. In recent decades, every single war has been ostensibly "justified." The *Catechism of the Catholic Church* speaks of the possibility of legitimate *defence* by means of military force, which involves demonstrating that certain "rigorous conditions of moral legitimacy"[239] have been met. Yet it is easy to fall into an overly broad interpretation of this potential right. In this way, some would also wrongly justify even "preventive" attacks or acts of war that can hardly avoid entailing "evils and disorders graver than the evil to be eliminated."[240] At issue is whether the development of nuclear, chemical and biological weapons, and the enormous and growing possibilities offered by new technologies, have granted war an uncontrollable destructive power over great numbers of innocent civilians. The truth is that "never has humanity had such power over itself, yet nothing ensures that it will be used wisely."[241] We can no longer think of war as a solution, because its risks will probably always

---

York (25 September 2015): AAS 107 (2015), 1041–1042.

239. No. 2309.

240. Ibid.

241. Encyclical Letter *Laudato Si'* (24 May 2015), 104: AAS 107 (2015), 888.

be greater than its supposed benefits. In view of this, it is very difficult nowadays to invoke the rational criteria elaborated in earlier centuries to speak of the possibility of a "just war." Never again war![242]

259. It should be added that, with increased globalization, what might appear as an immediate or practical solution for one part of the world initiates a chain of violent and often latent effects that end up harming the entire planet and opening the way to new and worse wars in the future. In today's world, there are no longer just isolated outbreaks of war in one country or another; instead, we are experiencing a "world war fought piecemeal," since the destinies of countries are so closely interconnected on the global scene.

260. In the words of Saint John XXIII, "it no longer makes sense to maintain that war is a fit instrument with which to repair the violation of justice."[243] In making this point amid great international tension, he voiced the growing desire for peace emerging in the Cold War period. He supported the conviction that the arguments for peace are stronger than any calculation of particular interests and confidence in the use of weaponry. The opportunities offered by the end of the Cold War were not, however, adequately seized due to a lack of a vision for the future and a shared consciousness of our common destiny. Instead, it proved easier to pursue partisan interests without upholding the universal common good. The dread spectre of war thus began to gain new ground.

261. Every war leaves our world worse than it was before. War is a failure of politics and of humanity, a shameful capitulation, a stinging defeat before the forces of evil. Let us not remain mired in theoretical discussions, but touch the wounded flesh of the victims. Let us look once more at all those civilians whose killing was considered "collateral damage." Let us ask the victims

242. Saint Augustine, who forged a concept of "just war" that we no longer uphold in our own day, also said that "it is a higher glory still to stay war itself with a word, than to slay men with the sword, and to procure or maintain peace by peace, not by war" (*Epistola* 229, 2: PL 33, 1020).

243. Encyclical Letter *Pacem in Terris* (11 April 1963): AAS 55 (1963), 291.

themselves. Let us think of the refugees and displaced, those who suffered the effects of atomic radiation or chemical attacks, the mothers who lost their children, and the boys and girls maimed or deprived of their childhood. Let us hear the true stories of these victims of violence, look at reality through their eyes, and listen with an open heart to the stories they tell. In this way, we will be able to grasp the abyss of evil at the heart of war. Nor will it trouble us to be deemed naive for choosing peace.

> "Every war leaves our world worse than it was before. War is a failure of politics and of humanity, a shameful capitulation, a stinging defeat before the forces of evil. Let us not remain mired in theoretical discussions, but touch the wounded flesh of the victims. Let us look once more at all those civilians whose killing was considered 'collateral damage.' Let us ask the victims themselves. Let us think of the refugees and displaced, those who suffered the effects of atomic radiation or chemical attacks, the mothers who lost their children, and the boys and girls maimed or deprived of their childhood. Let us hear the true stories of these victims of violence, look at reality through their eyes, and listen with an open heart to the stories they tell. In this way, we will be able to grasp the abyss of evil at the heart of war. Nor will it trouble us to be deemed naive for choosing peace" (no. 261).

262. Rules by themselves will not suffice if we continue to think that the solution to current problems is deterrence through fear or the threat of nuclear, chemical or biological weapons. Indeed, "if we take into consideration the principal threats to peace and security with their many dimensions in this multipolar world of the twenty-first century as, for example, terrorism, asymmetrical conflicts, cybersecurity, environmental problems, poverty,

not a few doubts arise regarding the inadequacy of nuclear deterrence as an effective response to such challenges. These concerns are even greater when we consider the catastrophic humanitarian and environmental consequences that would follow from any use of nuclear weapons, with devastating, indiscriminate and uncontainable effects, over time and space... We need also to ask ourselves how sustainable is a stability based on fear, when it actually increases fear and undermines relationships of trust between peoples. International peace and stability cannot be based on a false sense of security, on the threat of mutual destruction or total annihilation, or on simply maintaining a balance of power... In this context, the ultimate goal of the total elimination of nuclear weapons becomes both a challenge and a moral and humanitarian imperative... Growing interdependence and globalization mean that any response to the threat of nuclear weapons should be collective and concerted, based on mutual trust. This trust can be built only through dialogue that is truly directed to the common good and not to the protection of veiled or particular interests."[244] With the money spent on weapons and other military expenditures, let us establish a global fund[245] that can finally put an end to hunger and favour development in the most impoverished countries, so that their citizens will not resort to violent or illusory solutions, or have to leave their countries in order to seek a more dignified life.

The death penalty

263. There is yet another way to eliminate others, one aimed not at countries but at individuals. It is the death penalty. Saint John Paul II stated clearly and firmly that the death penalty is inadequate from a moral standpoint and no longer necessary from that of penal justice.[246] There can be no stepping back from

---

244. *Message to the United Nations Conference to Negotiate a Legally Binding Instrument to Prohibit Nuclear Weapons* (28 March 2017): AAS 109 (2017), 394–396.

245. Cf. Saint Paul VI, Encyclical Letter *Populorum Progressio* (26 March 1967): AAS 59 (1967), 282.

246. Cf. Encyclical Letter *Evangelium Vitae* (25 March 1995), 56: AAS 87 (1995), 463–464.

this position. Today we state clearly that "the death penalty is inadmissible"[247] and the Church is firmly committed to calling for its abolition worldwide.[248]

264. In the New Testament, while individuals are asked not to take justice into their own hands (cf. *Rom* 12:17.19), there is also a recognition of the need for authorities to impose penalties on evildoers (cf. *Rom* 13:4; *1 Pet* 2:14). Indeed, "civic life, structured around an organized community, needs rules of coexistence, the wilful violation of which demands appropriate redress."[249] This means that legitimate public authority can and must "inflict punishments according to the seriousness of the crimes"[250] and that judicial power be guaranteed a "necessary independence in the realm of law."[251]

265. From the earliest centuries of the Church, some were clearly opposed to capital punishment. Lactantius, for example, held that "there ought to be no exception at all; that it is always unlawful to put a man to death."[252] Pope Nicholas I urged that efforts be made "to free from the punishment of death not only each of the innocent, but all the guilty as well."[253] During the trial of the murderers of two priests, Saint Augustine asked the judge not to take the life of the assassins with this argument: "We do not object to your depriving these wicked men of the freedom to commit further crimes. Our desire is rather that justice be satisfied

247. *Address on the Twenty-fifth Anniversary of the Promulgation of the Catechism of the Catholic Church* (11 October 2017): AAS 109 (2017), 1196.

248. Cf. Congregation for the Doctrine of the Faith, *Letter to the Bishops Regarding the Revision of No. 2267 of the Catechism of the Catholic Church on the Death Penalty* (1 August 2018): *L'Osservatore Romano*, 3 August 2018, p. 8.

249. *Address to Delegates of the International Association of Penal Law* (23 October 2014): AAS 106 (2014), 840.

250. Pontifical Council for Justice and Peace, *Compendium of the Social Doctrine of the Church*, 402.

251. Saint John Paul II, *Address to the National Association of Magistrates* (31 March 2000), 4: AAS 92 (2000), 633.

252. *Divinae Institutiones* VI, 20, 17: PL 6, 708.

253. *Epistola 97 (Responsa ad consulta Bulgarorum)*, 25: PL 119, 991. "ipsi (Christo) non solum innoxios quosque, verum etiam et noxios a mortis exitio satagite cunctos eruere..."

without the taking of their lives or the maiming of their bodies in any part. And, at the same time, that by the coercive measures provided by the law, they be turned from their irrational fury to the calmness of men of sound mind, and from their evil deeds to some useful employment. This too is considered a condemnation, but who does not see that, when savage violence is restrained and remedies meant to produce repentance are provided, it should be considered a benefit rather than a mere punitive measure... Do not let the atrocity of their sins feed a desire for vengeance, but desire instead to heal the wounds which those deeds have inflicted on their souls."[254]

266. Fear and resentment can easily lead to viewing punishment in a vindictive and even cruel way, rather than as part of a process of healing and reintegration into society. Nowadays, "in some political sectors and certain media, public and private violence and revenge are incited, not only against those responsible for committing crimes, but also against those suspected, whether proven or not, of breaking the law... There is at times a tendency to deliberately fabricate enemies: stereotyped figures who represent all the characteristics that society perceives or interprets as threatening. The mechanisms that form these images are the same that allowed the spread of racist ideas in their time."[255] This has made all the more dangerous the growing practice in some countries of resorting to preventive custody, imprisonment without trial and especially the death penalty.

267. Here I would stress that "it is impossible to imagine that states today have no other means than capital punishment to protect the lives of other people from the unjust aggressor." Particularly serious in this regard are so-called extrajudicial or extralegal executions, which are "homicides deliberately committed by certain states and by their agents, often passed off as clashes with criminals or presented as the unintended consequences of the

254. *Epistola ad Marcellinum* 133, 1.2: PL 33, 509.

255. *Address to Delegates of the International Association of Penal Law* (23 October 2014): AAS 106 (2014), 840–841.

reasonable, necessary and proportionate use of force in applying the law."[256]

268. "The arguments against the death penalty are numerous and well-known. The Church has rightly called attention to several of these, such as the possibility of judicial error and the use made of such punishment by totalitarian and dictatorial regimes as a means of suppressing political dissidence or persecuting religious and cultural minorities, all victims whom the legislation of those regimes consider 'delinquents.' All Christians and people of good will are today called to work not only for the abolition of the death penalty, legal or illegal, in all its forms, but also to work for the improvement of prison conditions, out of respect for the human dignity of persons deprived of their freedom. I would link this to life imprisonment... A life sentence is a secret death penalty."[257]

> "The arguments against the death penalty are numerous and well-known. The Church has rightly called attention to several of these, such as the possibility of judicial error and the use made of such punishment by totalitarian and dictatorial regimes as a means of suppressing political dissidence or persecuting religious and cultural minorities, all victims whom the legislation of those regimes consider 'delinquents.' All Christians and people of good will are today called to work not only for the abolition of the death penalty, legal or illegal, in all its forms, but also to work for the improvement of prison conditions, out of respect for the human dignity of persons deprived of their freedom. I would link this to life imprisonment… A life sentence is a secret death penalty… Let us keep in mind that 'not even a murderer loses his personal dignity, and God himself

256. Ibid., 842.
257. Ibid.

> pledges to guarantee this.' The firm rejection of the death penalty shows to what extent it is possible to recognize the inalienable dignity of every human being and to accept that he or she has a place in this universe. If I do not deny that dignity to the worst of criminals, I will not deny it to anyone. I will give everyone the possibility of sharing this planet with me, despite all our differences" (nos. 268–69).

269. Let us keep in mind that "not even a murderer loses his personal dignity, and God himself pledges to guarantee this."[258] The firm rejection of the death penalty shows to what extent it is possible to recognize the inalienable dignity of every human being and to accept that he or she has a place in this universe. If I do not deny that dignity to the worst of criminals, I will not deny it to anyone. I will give everyone the possibility of sharing this planet with me, despite all our differences.

270. I ask Christians who remain hesitant on this point, and those tempted to yield to violence in any form, to keep in mind the words of the book of Isaiah: "They shall beat their swords into plowshares" (2:4). For us, this prophecy took flesh in Christ Jesus who, seeing a disciple tempted to violence, said firmly: "Put your sword back into its place; for all who take the sword will perish by the sword" (*Mt* 26:52). These words echoed the ancient warning: "I will require a reckoning for human life. Whoever sheds the blood of a man, by man shall his blood be shed" (Gen 9:5–6). Jesus' reaction, which sprang from his heart, bridges the gap of the centuries and reaches the present as an enduring appeal.

258. Saint John Paul II, Encyclical Letter *Evangelium Vitae* (25 March 1995), 9: AAS 87 (1995), 411.

QUESTIONS FOR REFLECTION AND DISCUSSION

1. As you meditate on this section focusing on forgiveness and reconciliation in paragraphs 236–45, what resonates with your own experiences—and why? What have you learned through your own efforts to forgive others and be forgiven by others? Who are the people who are hardest for you to forgive—and what does that reveal to you? How can these experiences serve as lessons, as well as sources for courage, compassion, and perseverance in order to address and resolve conflict or to right a wrong? How can we integrate forgiveness into more of our relationships, interactions, and communities?
2. Pope Francis invites us to think about the ways we undermine peace through "double-speak, hidden agendas and good manners that mask reality" (no. 226). In a social context where people might fear disagreement and appearing intolerant or judgmental, how do we resist the urge to simply avoid conflict or ignore the pain in and around us? How is the pope encouraging us to see conflict avoidance as a failure to hold together truth, mercy, and justice (no. 227)? If we hold together truth, mercy, and justice, what does it require that we think, feel, say, and do differently?
3. Pope Francis clarifies that forgiveness does not mean sacrificing accountability, or acquiescing to those who have or would "debase our dignity" (no. 241). How do you read this section in light of a Tradition that has sometimes prioritized the forgiveness of sins more than acknowledging, repenting, and atoning for them? What do you make of the fact that the pope does not appeal to the sacrament of reconciliation as a resource for the grace to be forgiven and to forgive others? How do you

think Christians can and should practice remorse without wallowing in our failures? How can we seek restoration without presuming it? How can we practice forgiveness without imposing it on others, especially the victim-survivors of grave sin?

4. War and peace can seem more like macro-level problems than personal concerns, which Pope Francis confronts directly: "Each of us should realize that 'even the harsh judgment I hold in my heart against my brother or my sister, the open wound that was never cured, the offense that was never forgiven, the rancor that is only going to hurt me, are all instances of a struggle that I carry within me, a little flame deep in my heart that needs to be extinguished before it turns into a great blaze'" (no. 243). How do we honor our feelings while also warding against being manipulated by blame and shame, suspicion and scorn, regret and bitterness? If we take seriously the idea that each one of us is called to be an "artisan of peace" (no. 284), what has to change in how we see God? Others? Ourselves? Where do you turn for hope that healing is possible, personally and collectively—and why?
5. In 2018, Pope Francis revised the *Catechism of the Catholic Church* to state that "'the death penalty is inadmissible because it is an attack on the inviolability and dignity of the person,' and she works with determination for its abolition worldwide" (no. 2267). Surveys show that the strongest proponents of the death penalty are Christians, even though Jesus was killed by capital punishment; how would you explain this? How do paragraphs 263–70 invite you to think more deeply about how we view criminal justice, and to do so in view of the cross (better thought of as the human response to God's love than God's response to human sin)?

FOR FURTHER READING

Ahern, Kevin. *Structures of Grace: Catholic Organizations Serving the Global Common Good*. Maryknoll, NY: Orbis Books, 2015.

Cahill, Lisa Sowle. *Blessed Are the Peacemakers: Pacifism, Just War, and Peacebuilding*. Minneapolis: Fortress Press, 2019.

Dear, John. *They Will Inherit the Earth: Peace & Nonviolence in a Time of Climate Change*. Maryknoll, NY: Orbis Books, 2018.

Doak, Mary. *A Prophetic, Public Church: Witness to Hope Amid the Global Crises of the Twenty-First Century*. Collegeville, MN: Liturgical Press, 2020.

Tutu, Desmond. *No Future without Forgiveness*. New York: Doubleday, 1999.

Chapter Eight

RELIGIONS AT THE SERVICE OF FRATERNITY IN OUR WORLD

SYNOPSIS

The final chapter of *Fratelli Tutti* underscores the social mission of the church as essential for witnessing the gospel, concentrating on interfaith solidarity as the culmination of dialogue, friendship, and "defending justice in society" (no. 271). By seeing people of faith—across various denominations and religions—as all children of God, we can "recognize one another as travelling companions, truly brothers and sisters" (no. 274). Ecumenism and interfaith exchange are incumbent upon our identity as a pilgrim people who are pressing onward, ever deeper, into the Holy Mystery we call God. These interreligious conversations and relationships keep us from settling on a "too small" idea of God, and to learn what God has revealed and is making possible outside our own tradition. This approach calls on us to see religious diversity not as a failure in fidelity (resulting from human finitude or sin) or the inevitable but perhaps lamentable consequence of diverse human belief and expression, but as part of God's multifaceted plan for salvation, one that seeks to include each and all. The church is a sacrament of this salvation at work in human history, "a family among families…open to bearing witness in today's world, open to faith hope and love for the Lord and for those whom he loves with a preferential love. A home with open doors. The Church is a home with open doors, because she is a mother" (no. 276). This is why Pope Francis argues that in the public realm, "room needs to be made for reflections born of religious traditions that are the repository of centuries of experience and wisdom," especially in the face of a secularized society that risks becoming distanced from religious values, preferring individualism and materialism instead of human dignity and the common good (no. 275).

We are reminded that "catholic" implies unity in diversity, a universality where "all things human are our concern" (no. 278). We can neither fence in our concern for others, nor our attentiveness and responsiveness to the presence and power of God at work in all times, all places, and with all peoples. *Fratelli Tutti* challenges us to grow our abilities in "loving and accepting all our brothers and sisters" not just in the abstract, but in confronting the causes of distrust and division (no. 86). This means working for the unity of all Christians (no. 280) and confronting the ways we fail in our essential duty to love God by loving our neighbor, perhaps by falling prey to "contempt, hatred, xenophobia or negation of others. The truth is that violence has no basis in our fundamental religious convictions, but only in their distortion" (no. 282). When religious belief becomes a reason for discrimination or terrorism, we have lost our way, unable to "recognize the fundamental values of our common humanity, values in the name of which we can and must cooperate, build and dialogue, pardon and grow; this will allow different voices to unite in creating a melody of sublime nobility and beauty, instead of fanatical cries of hatred" (no. 283).

Pope Francis invokes his own dialogue and interfaith collaboration with Grand Imam Ahmad Al-Tayyeb as the kind of encounter and solidarity that our world needs. Christians and Muslims make up well over half the global population and need to model fruitful exchanges that promote greater understanding, mutual respect across these traditions, and a shared commitment to eradicate violence.* In view of rising rates of anti-Semitism and Islamophobia, Christians must join with our Jewish and Muslim siblings in making known that religion should never be a reason to "incite war, hateful attitudes, hostility and extremism" or be used as a prop to excuse bloodshed of any kind. Pope Francis asserts, "God, the Almighty, has no need to be defended by anyone and does not want his name to be used to terrorize people" (no. 285).

The encyclical ends with a call to a "culture of dialogue," cooperation, and "reciprocal understanding as the method and standard" for an inclusive and equitable "culture of encounter" (no. 285). Pope Francis lifts up Martin Luther King, Desmond Tutu, and Mahatma Gandhi as non-Catholic examples (unfortunately, excluding any women from being recognized) of the solidarity modeled by St. Francis of Assisi and Blessed Charles de Foucauld. The latter is praised for his "total surrender to God towards an identification with the poor, abandoned in the depths of the African desert," who was martyred in the midst of his desire to live as a brother to all. Pope Francis concludes with "A Prayer to the Creator" and "An Ecumenical Christian Prayer," hoping they inspire in us a steadfast dedication to seeing others as our siblings

* For more on this topic, visit A Common Word, https://www.acommonword.com/.

and being siblings to them in return. "May God inspire that dream in each one of us. Amen" (no. 287).

---

271. The different religions, based on their respect for each human person as a creature called to be a child of God, contribute significantly to building fraternity and defending justice in society. Dialogue between the followers of different religions does not take place simply for the sake of diplomacy, consideration or tolerance. In the words of the Bishops of India, "the goal of dialogue is to establish friendship, peace and harmony, and to share spiritual and moral values and experiences in a spirit of truth and love."[259]

THE ULTIMATE FOUNDATION

272. As believers, we are convinced that, without an openness to the Father of all, there will be no solid and stable reasons for an appeal to fraternity. We are certain that "only with this awareness that we are not orphans, but children, can we live in peace with one another."[260] For "reason, by itself, is capable of grasping the equality between men and of giving stability to their civic coexistence, but it cannot establish fraternity."[261]

273. In this regard, I wish to cite the following memorable statement: "If there is no transcendent truth, in obedience to which man achieves his full identity, then there is no sure principle for guaranteeing just relations between people. Their self-interest as a class, group or nation would inevitably set them in opposition to one another. If one does not acknowledge transcendent truth, then the force of power takes over, and each person tends to make full use of the means at his disposal in order to impose his own

259. Catholic Bishops' Conference of India, *Response of the Church in India to the Present-day Challenges* (9 March 2016).

260. *Homily* at Mass in Domus Sanctae Marthae (17 May 2020).

261. Benedict XVI, Encyclical Letter *Caritas in Veritate* (29 June 2009), 19: AAS 101 (2009), 655.

interests or his own opinion, with no regard for the rights of others... The root of modern totalitarianism is to be found in the denial of the transcendent dignity of the human person who, as the visible image of the invisible God, is therefore by his very nature the subject of rights that no one may violate—no individual, group, class, nation or state. Not even the majority of the social body may violate these rights, by going against the minority."[262]

274. From our faith experience and from the wisdom accumulated over centuries, but also from lessons learned from our many weaknesses and failures, we, the believers of the different religions, know that our witness to God benefits our societies. The effort to seek God with a sincere heart, provided it is never sullied by ideological or self-serving aims, helps us recognize one another as travelling companions, truly brothers and sisters. We are convinced that "when, in the name of an ideology, there is an attempt to remove God from a society, that society ends up adoring idols, and very soon men and women lose their way, their dignity is trampled and their rights violated. You know well how much suffering is caused by the denial of freedom of conscience and of religious freedom, and how that wound leaves a humanity which is impoverished, because it lacks hope and ideals to guide it."[263]

275. It should be acknowledged that "among the most important causes of the crises of the modern world are a desensitized human conscience, a distancing from religious values and the prevailing individualism accompanied by materialistic philosophies that deify the human person and introduce worldly and material values in place of supreme and transcendental principles."[264] It is wrong when the only voices to be heard in public debate are those of the powerful and "experts." Room needs to be made for reflections born of religious traditions that are the repository of centuries of experience and wisdom. For "religious

262. Saint John Paul II, Encyclical Letter *Centesimus Annus* (1 May 1991), 44: AAS 83 (1991), 849.

263. *Address to the Leaders of Other Religions and Other Christian Denominations*, Tirana, Albania (21 September 2014): *Insegnamenti* II, 2 (2014), 277.

264. *Document on Human Fraternity for World Peace and Living Together*, Abu Dhabi (4 February 2019): *L'Osservatore Romano*, 4–5 February 2019, p. 6.

classics can prove meaningful in every age; they have an enduring power [to open new horizons, to stimulate thought, to expand the mind and the heart]." Yet often they are viewed with disdain as a result of "the myopia of a certain rationalism."[265]

276. For these reasons, the Church, while respecting the autonomy of political life, does not restrict her mission to the private sphere. On the contrary, "she cannot and must not remain on the sidelines" in the building of a better world, or fail to "reawaken the spiritual energy" that can contribute to the betterment of society.[266] It is true that religious ministers must not engage in the party politics that are the proper domain of the laity, but neither can they renounce the political dimension of life itself,[267] which involves a constant attention to the common good and a concern for integral human development. The Church "has a public role over and above her charitable and educational activities." She works for "the advancement of humanity and of universal fraternity."[268] She does not claim to compete with earthly powers, but to offer herself as "a family among families, this is the Church, open to bearing witness in today's world, open to faith hope and love for the Lord and for those whom he loves with a preferential love. A home with open doors. The Church is a home with open doors, because she is a mother."[269] And in imitation of Mary, the Mother of Jesus, "we want to be a Church that serves, that leaves home and goes forth from its places of worship, goes forth from its sacristies, in order to accompany life, to sustain hope, to be the sign of unity... to build bridges, to break down walls, to sow seeds of reconciliation."[270]

---

265. Apostolic Exhortation *Evangelii Gaudium* (24 November 2013), 256: AAS 105 (2013), 1123.

266. Benedict XVI, Encyclical Letter *Deus Caritas Est* (25 December 2005), 28: AAS 98 (2006), 240.

267. "Man is a political animal," Aristotle, *Politics*, 1253a 1–3.

268. Benedict XVI, Encyclical Letter *Caritas in Veritate* (29 June 2009), 11: AAS 101 (2009), 648.

269. *Address to the Catholic Community*, Rakovski, Bulgaria (6 May 2019): *L'Osservatore Romano*, 8 May 2019, p. 9.

270. *Homily*, Santiago de Cuba (22 September 2015): AAS 107 (2015), 1005.

Christian identity

277. The Church esteems the ways in which God works in other religions, and "rejects nothing of what is true and holy in these religions. She has a high regard for their manner of life and conduct, their precepts and doctrines which... often reflect a ray of that truth which enlightens all men and women."[271] Yet we Christians are very much aware that "if the music of the Gospel ceases to resonate in our very being, we will lose the joy born of compassion, the tender love born of trust, the capacity for reconciliation that has its source in our knowledge that we have been forgiven and sent forth. If the music of the Gospel ceases to sound in our homes, our public squares, our workplaces, our political and financial life, then we will no longer hear the strains that challenge us to defend the dignity of every man and woman."[272] Others drink from other sources. For us the wellspring of human dignity and fraternity is in the Gospel of Jesus Christ. From it, there arises, "for Christian thought and for the action of the Church, the primacy given to relationship, to the encounter with the sacred mystery of the other, to universal communion with the entire human family, as a vocation of all."[273]

"The Church esteems the ways in which God works in other religions, and 'rejects nothing of what is true and holy in these religions. She has a high regard for their manner of life and conduct, their precepts and doctrines which... often reflect a ray of that truth which enlightens all men and women.' Yet we Christians are very much aware that 'if the music of the Gospel ceases to resonate in our very being, we will lose the joy born of

271. Second Vatican Ecumenical Council, Declaration on the Relation of the Church to Non-Christian Religions *Nostra Aetate*, 2.

272. *Ecumenical Prayer Service*, Riga, Latvia (24 September 2018): *L'Osservatore Romano*, 24–25 September 2018, p. 8.

273. *Lectio Divina*, Pontifical Lateran University, Rome (26 March 2019): *L'Osservatore Romano*, 27 March 2019, p. 10.

compassion, the tender love born of trust, the capacity for reconciliation that has its source in our knowledge that we have been forgiven and sent forth. If the music of the Gospel ceases to sound in our homes, our public squares, our workplaces, our political and financial life, then we will no longer hear the strains that challenge us to defend the dignity of every man and woman.' Others drink from other sources. For us the wellspring of human dignity and fraternity is in the Gospel of Jesus Christ. From it, there arises, 'for Christian thought and for the action of the Church, the primacy given to relationship, to the encounter with the sacred mystery of the other, to universal communion with the entire human family, as a vocation of all'" (no. 277).

278. Called to take root in every place, the Church has been present for centuries throughout the world, for that is what it means to be "catholic." She can thus understand, from her own experience of grace and sin, the beauty of the invitation to universal love. Indeed, "all things human are our concern... wherever the councils of nations come together to establish the rights and duties of man, we are honoured to be permitted to take our place among them."[274] For many Christians, this journey of fraternity also has a Mother, whose name is Mary. Having received this universal motherhood at the foot of the cross (cf. *Jn* 19:26), she cares not only for Jesus but also for "the rest of her children" (cf. *Rev* 12:17). In the power of the risen Lord, she wants to give birth to a new world, where all of us are brothers and sisters, where there is room for all those whom our societies discard, where justice and peace are resplendent.

279. We Christians ask that, in those countries where we are a minority, we be guaranteed freedom, even as we ourselves

274. Saint Paul VI, Encyclical Letter *Ecclesiam Suam* (6 August 1964): AAS 56 (1964), 650.

promote that freedom for non-Christians in places where they are a minority. One fundamental human right must not be forgotten in the journey towards fraternity and peace. It is religious freedom for believers of all religions. That freedom proclaims that we can "build harmony and understanding between different cultures and religions. It also testifies to the fact that, since the important things we share are so many, it is possible to find a means of serene, ordered and peaceful coexistence, accepting our differences and rejoicing that, as children of the one God, we are all brothers and sisters."[275]

280. At the same time, we ask God to strengthen unity within the Church, a unity enriched by differences reconciled by the working of the Spirit. For "in the one Spirit we were all baptized into one body" (*1 Cor* 12:13), in which each member has his or her distinctive contribution to make. As Saint Augustine said, "the ear sees through the eye, and the eye hears through the ear."[276] It is also urgent to continue to bear witness to the journey of encounter between the different Christian confessions. We cannot forget Christ's desire "that they may all be one" (cf. *Jn* 17:21). Hearing his call, we recognize with sorrow that the process of globalization still lacks the prophetic and spiritual contribution of unity among Christians. This notwithstanding, "even as we make this journey towards full communion, we already have the duty to offer common witness to the love of God for all people by working together in the service of humanity."[277]

RELIGION AND VIOLENCE

281. A journey of peace is possible between religions. Its point of departure must be God's way of seeing things. "God does

275. *Address to the Civil Authorities*, Bethlehem, Palestine (25 May 2014): *Insegnamenti* II, 1 (2014), 597.

276. *Enarrationes in Psalmos*, 130, 6: PL 37, 1707.

277. *Common Declaration of Pope Francis and Ecumenical Patriarch Bartholomew*, Jerusalem (25 May 2014), 5: *L'Osservatore Romano*, 26–27 May 2014, p. 6

not see with his eyes, God sees with his heart. And God's love is the same for everyone, regardless of religion. Even if they are atheists, his love is the same. When the last day comes, and there is sufficient light to see things as they really are, we are going to find ourselves quite surprised."[278]

> "A journey of peace is possible between religions. Its point of departure must be God's way of seeing things. 'God does not see with his eyes, God sees with his heart. And God's love is the same for everyone, regardless of religion. Even if they are atheists, his love is the same. When the last day comes, and there is sufficient light to see things as they really are, we are going to find ourselves quite surprised'" (no. 281).

282. It follows that "we believers need to find occasions to speak with one another and to act together for the common good and the promotion of the poor. This has nothing to do with watering down or concealing our deepest convictions when we encounter others who think differently than ourselves... For the deeper, stronger and richer our own identity is, the more we will be capable of enriching others with our own proper contribution."[279] We believers are challenged to return to our sources, in order to concentrate on what is essential: worship of God and love for our neighbour, lest some of our teachings, taken out of context, end up feeding forms of contempt, hatred, xenophobia or negation of others. The truth is that violence has no basis in our fundamental religious convictions, but only in their distortion.

> "It follows that 'we believers need to find occasions to speak with one another and to act together for the

278. From the film *Pope Francis: A Man of His Word*, by Wim Wenders (2018).

279. Post-Synodal Apostolic Exhortation *Querida Amazonia* (2 February 2020), 106.

common good and the promotion of the poor. This has nothing to do with watering down or concealing our deepest convictions when we encounter others who think differently than ourselves... For the deeper, stronger and richer our own identity is, the more we will be capable of enriching others with our own proper contribution.' We believers are challenged to return to our sources, in order to concentrate on what is essential: worship of God and love for our neighbor, lest some of our teachings, taken out of context, end up feeding forms of contempt, hatred, xenophobia or negation of others. The truth is that violence has no basis in our fundamental religious convictions, but only in their distortion" (no. 282).

283. Sincere and humble worship of God "bears fruit not in discrimination, hatred and violence, but in respect for the sacredness of life, respect for the dignity and freedom of others, and loving commitment to the welfare of all."[280] Truly, "whoever does not love does not know God, for God is love" (*1 Jn* 4:8). For this reason, "terrorism is deplorable and threatens the security of people—be they in the East or the West, the North or the South—and disseminates panic, terror and pessimism, but this is not due to religion, even when terrorists instrumentalize it. It is due, rather, to an accumulation of incorrect interpretations of religious texts and to policies linked to hunger, poverty, injustice, oppression and pride. That is why it is so necessary to stop supporting terrorist movements fuelled by financing, the provision of weapons and strategy, and by attempts to justify these movements, even using the media. All these must be regarded as international crimes that threaten security and world peace. Such terrorism must be condemned in all its forms and expressions."[281]

280. *Homily*, Colombo, Sri Lanka (14 January 2015): AAS 107 (2015), 139.

281. *Document on Human Fraternity for World Peace and Living Together*, Abu Dhabi (4 February 2019): *L'Osservatore Romano*, 4–5 February 2019, p. 7.

Religious convictions about the sacred meaning of human life permit us "to recognize the fundamental values of our common humanity, values in the name of which we can and must cooperate, build and dialogue, pardon and grow; this will allow different voices to unite in creating a melody of sublime nobility and beauty, instead of fanatical cries of hatred."[282]

284. At times fundamentalist violence is unleashed in some groups, of whatever religion, by the rashness of their leaders. Yet, "the commandment of peace is inscribed in the depths of the religious traditions that we represent… As religious leaders, we are called to be true 'people of dialogue,' to cooperate in building peace not as intermediaries but as authentic mediators. Intermediaries seek to give everyone a discount, ultimately in order to gain something for themselves. The mediator, on the other hand, is one who retains nothing for himself, but rather spends himself generously until he is consumed, knowing that the only gain is peace. Each one of us is called to be an artisan of peace, by uniting and not dividing, by extinguishing hatred and not holding on to it, by opening paths of dialogue and not by constructing new walls."[283]

"As religious leaders, we are called to be true 'people of dialogue,' to cooperate in building peace not as intermediaries but as authentic mediators. Intermediaries seek to give everyone a discount, ultimately in order to gain something for themselves. The mediator, on the other hand, is one who retains nothing for himself, but rather spends himself generously until he is consumed, knowing that the only gain is peace. Each one of us is called to be an artisan of peace, by uniting and not dividing, by extinguishing hatred and not holding on to it, by

282. *Address to Civil Authorities*, Sarajevo, Bosnia-Herzegovina (6 June 2015): *L'Osservatore Romano*, 7 June 2015, p. 7.

283. *Address to the International Meeting for Peace organized by the Community of Sant'Egidio* (30 September 2013): *Insegnamenti* I, 1 (2013), 301–302.

opening paths of dialogue and not by constructing new walls" (no. 284).

An appeal

285. In my fraternal meeting, which I gladly recall, with the Grand Imam Ahmad Al-Tayyeb, "we resolutely [declared] that religions must never incite war, hateful attitudes, hostility and extremism, nor must they incite violence or the shedding of blood. These tragic realities are the consequence of a deviation from religious teachings. They result from a political manipulation of religions and from interpretations made by religious groups who, in the course of history, have taken advantage of the power of religious sentiment in the hearts of men and women... God, the Almighty, has no need to be defended by anyone and does not want his name to be used to terrorize people."[284] For this reason I would like to reiterate here the appeal for peace, justice and fraternity that we made together:

> "In the name of God, who has created all human beings equal in rights, duties and dignity, and who has called them to live together as brothers and sisters, to fill the earth and make known the values of goodness, love and peace;
>
> "In the name of innocent human life that God has forbidden to kill, affirming that whoever kills a person is like one who kills the whole of humanity, and that whoever saves a person is like one who saves the whole of humanity;
>
> "In the name of the poor, the destitute, the marginalized and those most in need, whom God has commanded us to help as a duty required of all persons, especially the wealthy and those of means;

284. *Document on Human Fraternity for World Peace and Living Together*, Abu Dhabi (4 February 2019): *L'Osservatore Romano*, 4–5 February 2019, p. 6.

"In the name of orphans, widows, refugees and those exiled from their homes and their countries; in the name of all victims of wars, persecution and injustice; in the name of the weak, those who live in fear, prisoners of war and those tortured in any part of the world, without distinction;

"In the name of peoples who have lost their security, peace and the possibility of living together, becoming victims of destruction, calamity and war;

"In the name of *human fraternity*, that embraces all human beings, unites them and renders them equal;

"In the name of this *fraternity* torn apart by policies of extremism and division, by systems of unrestrained profit or by hateful ideological tendencies that manipulate the actions and the future of men and women;

"In the name of freedom, that God has given to all human beings, creating them free and setting them apart by this gift;

"In the name of justice and mercy, the foundations of prosperity and the cornerstone of faith;

"In the name of all persons of goodwill present in every part of the world;

"In the name of God and of everything stated thus far, [we] declare the adoption of a culture of dialogue as the path; mutual cooperation as the code of conduct; reciprocal understanding as the method and standard."[285]

"In my fraternal meeting, which I gladly recall, with the Grand Imam Ahmad Al-Tayyeb, 'we resolutely [declared] that religions must never incite war, hateful attitudes, hostility and extremism, nor must they incite violence

285. Ibid.

> or the shedding of blood. These tragic realities are the consequence of a deviation from religious teachings. They result from a political manipulation of religions and from interpretations made by religious groups who, in the course of history, have taken advantage of the power of religious sentiment in the hearts of men and women... God, the Almighty, has no need to be defended by anyone and does not want his name to be used to terrorize people'" (no. 285).

* * *

286. In these pages of reflection on universal fraternity, I felt inspired particularly by Saint Francis of Assisi, but also by others of our brothers and sisters who are not Catholics: Martin Luther King, Desmond Tutu, Mahatma Gandhi and many more. Yet I would like to conclude by mentioning another person of deep faith who, drawing upon his intense experience of God, made a journey of transformation towards feeling a brother to all. I am speaking of Blessed Charles de Foucauld.

287. Blessed Charles directed his ideal of total surrender to God towards an identification with the poor, abandoned in the depths of the African desert. In that setting, he expressed his desire to feel himself a brother to every human being,[286] and asked a friend to "pray to God that I truly be the brother of all."[287] He wanted to be, in the end, "the universal brother."[288] Yet only by identifying with the least did he come at last to be the brother of all. May God inspire that dream in each one of us. Amen.

---

286. Cf. Charles de Foucauld, *Méditation sur le Notre Père* (23 January 1897).

287. *Letter to Henry de Castries* (29 November 1901).

288. *Letter to Madame de Bondy* (7 January 1902). Saint Paul VI used these words in praising his commitment: Encyclical Letter *Populorum Progressio* (26 March 1967): AAS 59 (1967), 263.

A Prayer to the Creator

Lord, Father of our human family,
you created all human beings equal in dignity:
pour forth into our hearts a fraternal spirit
and inspire in us a dream of renewed encounter,
dialogue, justice and peace.
Move us to create healthier societies
and a more dignified world,
a world without hunger, poverty, violence and war.

May our hearts be open
to all the peoples and nations of the earth.
May we recognize the goodness and beauty
that you have sown in each of us,
and thus forge bonds of unity, common projects,
and shared dreams. Amen.

An Ecumenical Christian Prayer

O God, Trinity of love,
from the profound communion of your divine life,
pour out upon us a torrent of fraternal love.
Grant us the love reflected in the actions of Jesus,
in his family of Nazareth,
and in the early Christian community.

Grant that we Christians may live the Gospel,
discovering Christ in each human being,
recognizing him crucified
in the sufferings of the abandoned
and forgotten of our world,
and risen in each brother or sister
who makes a new start.

Come, Holy Spirit, show us your beauty,
reflected in all the peoples of the earth,
so that we may discover anew

that all are important and all are necessary,
different faces of the one humanity
that God so loves. Amen.

QUESTIONS FOR REFLECTION AND DISCUSSION

1. What experience do you have with people of other faith traditions? What have you learned from them about who God is and what God wants for and from us? As you review this section of the encyclical (especially no. 285), how do you think non-Catholics or non-Christians might add to your sense of what God is doing in the world, and the gifts we can be to one another, in our respective dignity and freedom?
2. The pope quotes the bishops of India in saying, "The goal of dialogue is to establish friendship, peace and harmony, and to share spiritual and moral values and experiences in a spirit of truth and love" (no. 271). How has this encyclical encouraged and challenged you to hold together truth and love, including by engaging others across differences? What, from this document, might you try to remember or reference in the event you feel anxious, defensive, or even combative when encountering people of different beliefs and values? How can you model robust dialogue with your family and friends, your neighbors and coworkers, and with people of other faiths? How can your local faith community put the spirit of *Fratelli Tutti* to work with other local faith communities? What difference might this make for the people involved?
3. *Fratelli Tutti* highlights the social mission of the church by saying, "The Church, while respecting the autonomy of political life, does not restrict her mission to the private

sphere. On the contrary, 'she cannot and must not remain on the sidelines' in the building of a better world, or fail to 'reawaken the spiritual energy' that can contribute to the betterment of society" (no. 276). What might keep you and your local faith community on the sidelines in the work to defend human dignity, deliver on human rights, and promote the common good? How can such efforts be framed as fidelity to God and neighbor, not as partisan or "getting political" and thus alienating members of the community? What are the human needs that call to your heart—and how can you invite others to join you in responding to them?

4. Pope Francis calls each one of us to be an "artisan of peace," to see our place in the world as a workshop for hope and healing (no. 284). How can you bring this artisanship to your relationships, as a mediator working to bring people and groups together?
5. This encyclical calls on us to "dream together" (no. 8), by tapping into our deepest desires for ourselves and our world. What do you most deeply desire for yourself in light of what you have read—and why? What do you most deeply desire for your local faith community—and why? What do you most deeply desire for the broader community where you live—and why? What is your prayer—and what will be your action—for what can become possible through you in the days ahead? In light of the last step in the pastoral spiral—evaluation—how will you assess the effectiveness of your goals and strategies? What wisdom and encouragement can you receive from and offer others?

FOR FURTHER READING

Duffner, Jordan Denari. *Islamophobia: What Christians Should Know (and Do) about Anti-Muslim Discrimination*. Maryknoll, NY: Orbis Books, 2021.

Massingale, Bryan N. *Racial Justice and the Catholic Church*. Maryknoll, NY: Orbis Books, 2010.

Phan, Peter C. *The Joy of Religious Pluralism: A Personal Journey*. Maryknoll, NY: Orbis Books, 2017.

Schreiter, Robert J. *The New Catholicity: Theology between the Global and the Local*. Maryknoll, NY: Orbis Books, 1997.

Sweeney, Jon M., ed. *Jesus Wasn't Killed by the Jews: Reflections for Christians in Lent*. Maryknoll, NY: Orbis Books, 2020.

RESOURCES

BOOKS

Ahlgren, Gillian T. W. *The Tenderness of God: Reclaiming Our Humanity*. Minneapolis: Fortress Press, 2017.

Brackley, Dean. *The Call to Discernment in Troubled Times*. New York: Crossroad, 2004.

Brady, Bernard V. *Be Good & Do Good: Thinking Through Moral Theology*. Maryknoll, NY: Orbis Books, 2014.

Camosy, Charles C. *Resisting Throwaway Culture: How a Consistent Life Ethic Can Unite a Fractured People*. Hyde Park, NY: New City Press, 2019.

Clark, Meghan J. *The Vision of Catholic Social Thought: The Virtue of Solidarity and the Praxis of Human Rights*. Minneapolis: Fortress Press, 2014.

Donahue, John R. *Seek Justice that You May Live: Reflections and Resources on the Bible and Social Justice*. New York: Paulist Press, 2014.

Dunson, Donald H., and James A. Dunson III. *Citizen of the World: Suffering and Solidarity in the 21st Century*. Maryknoll, NY: Orbis Books, 2013.

Eggemeier, Matthew T., and Peter Joseph Fritz. *The Politics of Mercy: Catholic Life in an Era of Inequality, Racism, and Violence*. New York: Herder & Herder, 2020.

Francis, Pope. *The Church of Mercy: A Vision for the Church*. Chicago: Loyola Press, 2014.

———. *Let Us Dream: The Path to a Better Future*. New York: Simon & Schuster, 2020.

———. *The Name of God is Mercy*. New York: Random House, 2016.

Gutiérrez, Gustavo, and Cardinal Gerhard Ludwig Müller. *On the Side of the Poor: The Theology of Liberation*. Maryknoll, NY: Orbis Books, 2015.

John of Taizé, Brother. *Friends in Christ: Paths to a New Understanding of Church*. Maryknoll, NY: Orbis Books, 2012.

Kammer, Fred. *Doing Faithjustice: An Introduction to Catholic Social Thought*. Mahwah, NJ: Paulist Press, 2004.

Lennan, Richard, and Nancy Pineda-Madrid. *Hope: Promise, Possibility, and Fulfillment*. Mahwah, NJ: Paulist Press, 2013.

Markey, John J. *Moses in Pharaoh's House: A Liberation Spirituality for North America*. Winona, MN: Anselm Academic, 2014.

Massaro, Thomas. *Living Justice: Catholic Social Teaching in Action*. 3rd ed. Lanham, MD: Rowman & Littlefield, 2016.

———. *Mercy in Action: The Social Teachings of Pope Francis*. Lanham, MD: Rowman & Littlefield, 2018.

Massingale, Bryan N. *Racial Justice and the Catholic Church*. Maryknoll, NY: Orbis Books, 2010.

Merton, Thomas. *New Seeds of Contemplation*. New York: New Directions, 1961.

Mescher, Marcus. *The Ethics of Encounter: Christian Neighbor Love as a Practice of Solidarity*. Maryknoll, NY: Orbis Books, 2020.

O'Connell, Maureen H. *Compassion: Loving Our Neighbor in an Age of Globalization*. Maryknoll, NY: Orbis Books, 2009.

Pope, Stephen J. *A Step Along the Way: Models of Christian Service*. Maryknoll, NY: Orbis Books, 2015.

Pramuk, Christopher. *Hope Sings, So Beautiful: Graced Encounters across the Color Line*. Collegeville, MN: Liturgical Press, 2013.

Riccardi, Andrea. *To the Margins: Pope Francis and the Mission of the Church*. Maryknoll, NY: Orbis, 2018.

Smith, Gary. *Radical Compassion: Finding Christ in the Heart of the Poor*. Chicago: Loyola Press, 2002.

Spohn, William C. *Go and Do Likewise: Jesus and Ethics*. New York: Continuum, 2006.

Vasko, Elisabeth T. *Beyond Apathy: A Theology for Bystanders*. Minneapolis: Fortress Press, 2015.

Wall, Barbara E., and Massimo Faggioli. *Pope Francis: A Voice for Mercy, Justice, Love, and Care for the Earth*. Maryknoll: NY, Orbis Books, 2019.

WEBSITES

Bread for the World: https://www.bread.org/

Catholic Campaign for Human Development: https://www.usccb.org/committees/catholic-campaign-human-development

Catholic Charities: https://www.catholiccharitiesusa.org/

Catholic Climate Covenant: https://catholicclimatecovenant.org/

Catholic Mobilizing Network: https://catholicsmobilizing.org/

Catholic Relief Services: https://www.crs.org/

Churches for Middle East Peace: https://cmep.org/

Creation Justice Ministries: https://www.creationjustice.org/

Education for Justice: https://educationforjustice.org/

Equal Justice USA: https://ejusa.org/

Franciscan Action Network: https://franciscanaction.org/

Global Catholic Climate Movement: https://catholicclimatemovement.global/

Hope Border Institute: https://www.hopeborder.org/
Human Thread Campaign: http://www.humanthreadcampaign.org/
Jesuit Refugee Service: https://www.jrsusa.org/
JustFaith Ministries: https://justfaith.org/
Kino Border Initiative: https://www.kinoborderinitiative.org/
Maryknoll Office for Global Concerns: https://maryknollogc.org/
Pax Christi USA: https://paxchristiusa.org/
Poor People's Campaign: https://www.poorpeoplescampaign.org/
Showing Up for Racial Justice: https://www.showingupforracialjustice.org/
U.S. Catholic Sisters against Human Trafficking: https://sistersagainsttrafficking.org/
USCCB Justice for Immigrants: https://justiceforimmigrants.org/